Reflections of

SCOTLAND

To Russell Thomson, who first showed me mountains.

First published in Great Britain in 2009 by
Lomond Books Ltd., Broxburn, EH52 5NF, Scotland

www.lomondbooks.com

This edition 2018

Copyright © Lomond Books Ltd 2015

Text by Julie Davidson,
Copyright © Lomond Books Ltd 2015

Photographs © 2013 by:

Colin Baxter: Pages: 3, 6, 8, 15, 16, 17, 22, 32, 43, 44, 47, 49, 51, 60, 65, 92, 94, 95, 97, 98, 103, 107, 112, 113, 128, 129, 138, 139, 154.

Laurie Campbell: Pages: 1, 20, 21, 24, 26, 27, 50, 74, 81, 114, 152, 153.

Allan Devlin: Pages: 37, 40, 41, 42.

Alan Gordon: Pages: 79, 104.

Dennis Hardley: Pages: front cover, 4, 11, 12, 18, 25, 31, 39, 48, 53, 54, 55, 62, 67, 68, 70, 71, 72, 75, 76, 77, 82, 83, 84, 88, 90, 99, 121, 136.

Doug Houghton: Pages: 106, 150, 158.

Duncan McEwan: Pages: 28, 36, 38, 52, 61, 89, 100, 108, 109, 117, 118, 134, 137.

John MacPherson: Pages: 66, 151, 160.

David Robertson: Pages: 34, 35, 58, 59, 78, 87, 91, 123, 131, 143, 157, 159.

Iain Sarjeant: Pages: back cover, 73, 80, 115, 124, 125, 126, 127, 132, 133, 135, 140, 144, 145, 146, 147, 148, 149, 156.

Glyn Satterley: Pages: 56, 111.

Michael Stirling-Aird: Page: 19.

A CIP catalogue record for this book is available from the British Library

ISBN 978-1-84204-182-6

Printed in China

Front cover: *Kilchurn Castle, Loch Awe*   Page 1: *Highland Cow*   Page 3: *Isle of Arran.*   Back cover: *Torridon, Wester Ross*

Reflections of
SCOTLAND

text by Julie Davidson

LOMOND

A traditional crofthouse in Argyll; the tin roof has replaced what would have been a thatch of turf with cereal straw or reed.

Contents

Reflections of Scotland

INTRODUCTION

Scotland in the 21st century. "Stands Scotland where it did?" demanded Macduff, as he prepared to overthrow the tyrant Macbeth in the penultimate act of Shakespeare's tragedy. Not exactly. We have been spared tyrants but we have consolidated constitutional change since I last wrote some reflections on what to expect of this beguiling, disputatious, warm-hearted but prickly little country, which one literary tourist, Sydney Smith, sneeringly dubbed "the knuckle-end of England" and another, Henry James, called "beautiful and admirable – once you get the hang of it".

Everyone has an opinion on Scotland, most of all the Scots, and in the decade since the turn of the century the nation's altered status – a recovered if limited form of self-government – has been the focus of vigorous debate, often in tandem with the merits and demerits of its costliest new visitor attraction: Holyrood, the purpose-built home of the re-constituted Scottish parliament – quite possibly the most controversial building in our history since

Hadrian threw a wall across the north of England to keep the Picts in their place.

Love it or hate it, the complex building, lavishly accessorised with granite, oak and glass, has transformed the east end of Edinburgh's Royal Mile, not to mention the views from the neighbourhood hills. In fact, it is only possible to get an overview of its quirky design from the heights of Arthur's Seat. Walk up the Radical Road from Holyrood Park – a steep but easily navigated track beneath Salisbury Crag – and you will see where much of the money (£414 million) went and form your own opinion of its architectural quality.

If the parliament building has now settled into the capital cityscape the Scottish appetite for argument has not subsided. The comic tale is told of the Scotsman who struggled ashore from a shipwreck and found himself on an unknown island; unknown but not uninhabited. "Do you have a government here?" is his first question to the locals. When they tell him yes, they do have a

Castle Stalker stands on an islet at the mouth of Loch Laoich, off Loch Linnhe. It was built around 1540 by the Stewarts of Appin and is now privately owned.

government he responds smartly: "Well, I'm agin it."

There's only one thing we enjoy more than being contrary: taking sides in arguments which are centuries old. Recently Scotland commemorated the birth anniversaries of two controversial figures: Robert Burns, icon of the literary and drinking classes, and John Calvin, the French Protestant Reformer whose doctrines so influenced our own John Knox that the word Calvinist – perhaps unjustly – has come to signify all that is repressive in Scottish Presbyterianism.

Burns, the Ayrshire "ploughman poet" whose lyrical love poems and comic satires turned him into a cult figure at home and gave him an international reputation, was born in 1759. Calvin was born 250 years earlier. Each has a reputation burdened with much prejudicial baggage, not to mention anecdotal rumour, and each has come to symbolise the polar opposites of the Scottish character – or, at least, how they are popularly perceived.

Burns bears the standard for all that is romantic, feckless, philandering and bibulous in our genes, but is excused for his creative genius. Calvin and Knox are supposed to represent all that is dour, buttoned-up, austere and judgmental in our nature, and is condemned for undermining our self-esteem and social confidence. History and its myth-makers have often mis-represented

them, but they have this in common: their legacies remain so vigorous that they continue to inspire popular analysis – fireside arguments and pub debates, if you like – as much as new works of literary and theological research.

The letters pages of two of Scotland's leading quality newspapers, *The Scotsman* and *The Herald*, routinely reveal the contentious nature of Scots, and our endless fascination with the people who have been large figures on our landscape and the influences which have shaped us. New visitors may not have current affairs and contemporary issues high on their list of priorities as they travel the country of their guide books, but these newspapers are worth a glance for those interested in adding modern voices to their Scottish experience; which, as this book acknowledges, will almost certainly seek to embrace the rich history, celebrated traditions, magnificent scenery and cultural highlights which are the bread and butter of our tourist industry.

Our chattering classes have long girned – "girning" being the old Scots verb for complaining – that the emblems of that industry not only distort the realities of 21st-century Scotland but also misrepresent our past. By that they mean there is too much emphasis on kilts, whisky, heather and bagpipes, warrior heroes and tragic queens; not to mention a certain mysterious behemoth whose presence, in the lightless depths of a Highland loch, has never been

The Scottish Parliament building was completed in 2004. It occupies a site at the bottom of the Royal Mile between two of Edinburgh's landmark hills, Arthur's Seat and Calton Hill.

established, but who exercises such fascination that the Loch Ness Monster has created its own micro-industry.

This marketing mix is no recent concept; it dates back to the historical novels and romantic poetry of Sir Walter Scott, who first presented "brave Caledonia" to an international readership, and "Balmorality" – the enthusiasm for all things piped and kilted which followed Queen Victoria to her holiday home in the Dee Valley. But if too much tartan (which until the 19th century was the traditional cloth of only the Highland clans) has been wrapped around Scotland's identity, at least the process has given the nation a brand recognisable all over the world; a kind of corporate logo which signals our difference from other parts of the United Kingdom.

The receptive tourist will soon find there is more to Scotland than its myths and stereotypes, and thus much more to discover and enjoy. *Reflections of Scotland*, like reflections in a mirror of water, gives only a partial impression of the bigger picture. The book doesn't aspire to be comprehensive, or to catalogue all or even most of Scotland's achievements, attractions and interests, past or present. It is, rather, an attempt to give atmosphere and texture to the country's regions through its images and text, and to give visitors some modest prompts to their enjoyment of the Hebrides or Borders, Lowlands or Highlands.

It is not a castle-by-castle guide or a gazette of star-rated listings but an effort to distil the essence of Scotland's different parts, fortified by information on some of its most colourful or dramatic elements: clans and tartan, whisky and golf, castles and abbeys, poets, monsters and massacres. Here, too, are brief profiles of the ancient peoples, Celts, Picts, Angles, Gaels, who came together to forge a nation, and the contribution made by Scotland's Norse colonies and Viking past. And here is a short explanation of the rise and fall of the *Gaedhealechd* – the Gaelic-speaking regions of the Highlands and Islands which suffered most from oppression and displacement in the events which followed the creation of the British state in 1707.

First-time visitors will have their own preconceptions and expectations of Sir Walter Scott's "land of the mountain and the flood". Some of them will be overturned, many of them will be met. But I defy anyone to be disappointed by Scotland's landscape – its elusive, ever-changing qualities of light and shade, spectacle and detail, reflected in all their grimness and glory by the photographs in this book. Scotland is a visual feast, a never-ending banquet of ocular sensations. This is merely the taster menu.

Julie Davidson

Despite their proximity to urban Scotland and the Glasgow conurbation, Loch Lomond and its famous "bonnie banks" are Highland in character and – at day's end – tranquil in mood.

Seats of Power

SOUTHEASTERN SCOTLAND

Edinburgh, wrote the novelist Charlotte Bronte in a rapture of literary imagery, is "a lyric, brief, bright, clear and vital as a flash of lightning". She was not the first writer overwhelmed by her introduction to this strange, precipitous, beautiful but austere capital, which in the age known as the Scottish Enlightenment – the mid-18th to mid-19th centuries – was a European centre of excellence for science, philosophy, literature and publishing. This was the period when Edinburgh became two cities: the Georgian New Town and the medieval Old Town, each miraculously extant (more or less) today.

They face each other across the green valley of Princes Street Gardens and remain the heart of the city. With a few unhappy exceptions they have been well conserved, and the quality of their architecture has earned them World Heritage status. They have also become symbols of what has been called Edinburgh's "duality": the split personalities of its physical character, and perhaps its soul; one fair and civilised, the other dark and brutish – just like Dr Jekyll and Mr Hyde, the invention of Edinburgh-born Robert Louis Stevenson.

The aspirational New Town is Dr Jekyll. Its 18th-century design by James Craig, embellished by Robert Adam, is rational, harmonious, with broad thoroughfares and elegant squares and crescents. Here you can imagine bumping into the philosopher David Hume, the economist Adam Smith, the poet Alan Ramsay or Sir Walter Scott, whose first married home in Castle Street may be one of many dignified Georgian town houses, but is more soothing to the eye than the blackened Gothic spike which the Victorians raised to his memory at the east end of Princes Street Gardens.

The Old Town is Mr Hyde. It sits on a volcanic ridge between the Castle Rock and Holyrood Park, whose centrepiece is the mini-mountain called Arthur's Seat. Medieval Edinburgh is a place of cliffs and chasms, narrow, shadowy passageways called "closes", steep steps and towering tenements. Its spine is the Royal Mile, so called for its route from Edinburgh Castle to the Palace of Holyroodhouse – the royal residence most intimately associated with Mary Queen of Scots, who witnessed the murder of her favourite musician, David Rizzio, in one of its rooms.

You can walk from the southern edge of the Old Town to the northern fringe of the New Town in 40 minutes and find – in this heartland of the annual Edinburgh International Festival

"Stately Edinburgh throned on crags", according to William Wordsmith. In certain lights Edinburgh's 11th-century castle and its volcanic rock seem part of an organic whole.

– almost everything you want to know and enjoy: galleries, museums, shops, monuments, restaurants, bars, bus and railway stations. The city centre is wonderfully compact and a pedestrian's nirvana, full of interest and surprise, quirky corners, noble buildings and sudden views to hill and water. Edinburgh seems almost an organic extension of its rising site between the Firth of Forth and the Pentland Hills, and even in the worst weather never lacks atmosphere.

Opposite the new parliament building at the bottom of the Royal Mile is a pretty courtyard called Whitehorse Close, once the terminus of the London-Edinburgh stagecoach. The capital's southeast hinterland, Lothian and the Borders, has been the gateway to and from England for centuries, and usually first in the firing line of any invading army. The countryside which straddles the Tweed Valley and the frontier with England from Berwick-on-Tweed to the Solway Firth was long known as the "debatable lands"; national interests collided and local warlords fought over its possession, and the town of Berwick was batted between the two nations 13 times between 1147 and 1482 before it was finally claimed by England; although – an anomaly which demonstrates the robust identity of Borderers, many of whom see themselves as neither Scots nor English – its local football team plays in the Scottish league.

Border families were infamous not only for their blood feuds but for the cross-Border raids on cattle and property of the "reivers" – the old Scots word for plunderers. Its stormy past has stocked the region with much to explore, from gaunt and desolate fortresses to the romantic ruins of its great abbeys. Its landscape of lonely, sheep-cropped hills, wooded river valleys and rugged seaboard is full of character, and as its wildness became tamed, civilisation arrived in the form of handsome little towns like Kelso, Peebles and Melrose, magnificent Georgian "palaces" like Bowhill House, Floors Castle and Mellerstain, homes of Borders nobility, and the woollen industry powered by the River Tweed. The novels of Sir Walter Scott and John Buchan are much influenced by their years in the Borders, and there are literary shrines to both at Abbotsford House (Scott's home from 1811 to 1832) and the John Buchan Centre at Broughton, the village where Buchan grew up.

As you travel towards Edinburgh the debatable lands ease into one of Scotland's comeliest counties: East Lothian, where rich, rolling farmland meets the beaches, bays and championship golf courses of the Forth littoral. Here are some of the Southeast's most attractive villages and small towns: North Berwick, Dirleton, Aberlady and, inland, Haddington and Gifford. East Lothian also has its share of castles – most spectacularly Tantallon, on the cliffs between North Berwick and Dunbar – and the seabird-crowded Forth islands, including the mighty Bass Rock, can be inspected on boat trips from North Berwick. Due south of Edinburgh, in neighbouring Midlothian, is one of the most visited sites in the country: Rosslyn Chapel. With its elaborate stone carvings and enigmatic emblems this 15th-century burial place of the Sinclair family achieved popular global celebrity through the novel and film *The Da Vinci Code*.

Bringing the age of the train to the Forth estuary, the Forth Bridge is a mighty feat of Victorian engineering and was the longest bridge in the world when it was completed in 1890.

Edinburgh City Centre, where Old Town and New Town face each other across Princes Street Gardens.
Edinburgh's Georgian New Town (opposite) exemplifies the rational mood of the late 18th century which influenced James Craig's design.

Tyninghame Beach, a beguiling stretch of the East Lothian coast between North Berwick and Dunbar.
Tantallon Castle and the Bass Rock (opposite): fortresses – man-made and natural – of the Firth of Forth.

St Abb's Head, in Berwickshire, is a nature reserve for one of Scotland's most important seabird colonies.
"Scott's View" over the River Tweed and Eildon Hills (opposite) was a favourite spot of the writer Sir Walter Scott.

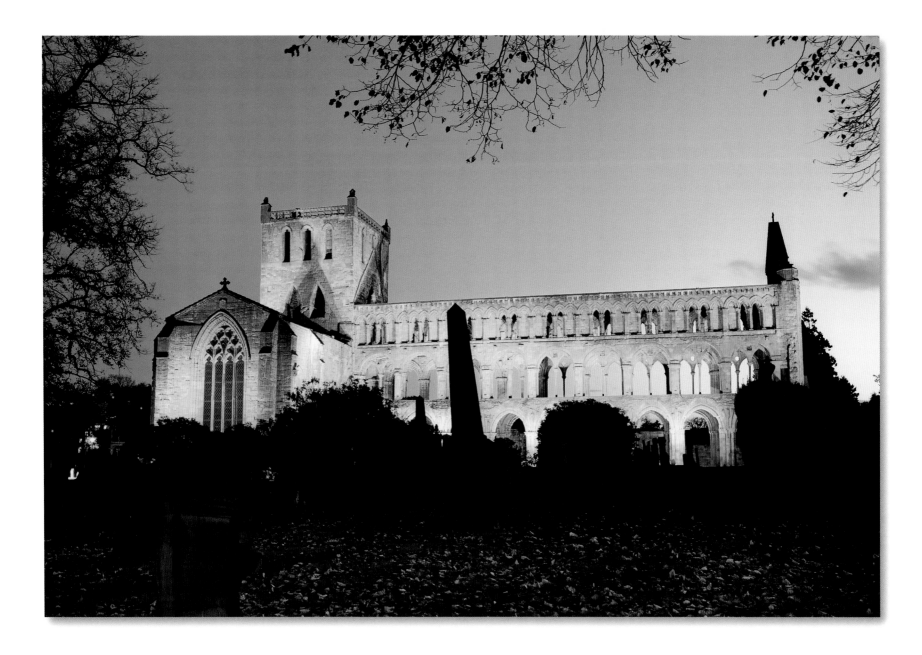

Jedburgh Abbey, one of three 12th-century Border abbeys founded by the pious and influential King David I.

The Border Abbeys

The malevolent ghost of Henry VIII stalks the empty naves and shattered walls of the four 12th-century Border abbeys: Jedburgh, Dryburgh, Melrose and Kelso, splendid ruins which have acquired a dignity that defies their lost purpose. England's wife-swapping Tudor king has become almost a comic figure in popular culture for the brevity of his marital attention-span – and his bloodthirsty option to the quickie divorce – but he was a violent and vindictive man. When the Scottish government, led by Cardinal Beaton and Mary of Guise, mother of Mary Queen of Scots, resisted his efforts to broker a marriage between his son Edward and the infant Mary (a union which would have dissolved the "Auld Alliance" between Scotland and France and given Henry a stranglehold on Scotland) he pursued a policy of "rough wooing", as it came to be called. His armies rampaged through the Borders with sword and torch and the great abbeys fell.

Three of them are embedded in their venerable towns, but Dryburgh's setting is pastoral and stands among trees beside the River Tweed. The most complete of the quartet, it was founded in 1150, probably by Sir Hugh de Montford, Constable of Scotland. Successive assaults by the English reached their climax in 1544, when it became another casualty of Henry's Rough Wooing. In the early 1700s the abbey lands belonged to the great-grandfather of Sir Walter Scott, and even when they had passed out of their hands the family retained the right to "stretch their bones" there. The writer is buried in the abbey church, and it's said that when the mile-long cortège was on its way from Abbotsford the horses automatically stopped at Sir Walter's favourite view of the triple peaks of the Eildon Hills, now called "Scott's View".

The abbeys of Jedburgh, Melrose and Kelso all owe their existence to one of Scotland's most pious and influential kings: David I. The oldest is Kelso, which David established in 1128, and its remnants are sparse. What remains – a mixture of Norman and Gothic styles – is only the West end of what was a monumental church, which claimed precedence over St Andrews. Its definitive catastrophe arrived in 1545 with one of Henry's generals, who found the abbey garrisoned, killed all defenders, including 12 monks, and razed the buildings.

Melrose Abbey belongs to the Borders' most picturesque town, which lies at the foot of the Eildon Hills. It was founded in 1136 for Cistercian monks from Rievaulx, in Yorkshire, and was a successor to the 7th-century monastery of Old Melrose. It sits in peaceful gardens between the Eildon slopes, the small town centre and the Tweed, and despite the fact that it was repeatedly wrecked over four centuries and then used for building material, some of its elaborate stonework and fine carvings have survived. The abbey is more popularly famous for its claim on the heart of Robert the Bruce, who restored it in 1326 after the first English demolition and bequeathed his vital organ to his handiwork. It, too, was destroyed and abandoned in 1545, after another bout of Rough Wooing.

The town of Jedburgh is only 10 miles from the thrilling Border crossing of Carter Bar, a high gateway in the Cheviot Hills. Its abbey dominates an early Christian site above the Jed Water and was originally a priory, founded in 1138, which achieved abbey status nine years later. It, too, endured the usual cycle of English sacking and Scots restoration until it was finally destroyed between 1544 and 1545. It should be added that, from the 16th century onwards, the neglect of all these noble buildings was down to Scotland's Protestant Reformation, which was not kind to Catholic churches and expunged their statuary and works of art. The Reformers also requisitioned the buildings for their new form of worship, and part of Jedburgh's nave was used as the parish church until 1875.

Traquair House was originally built as a royal hunting lodge before 1107 and is probably the oldest inhabited house in Scotland.
Kelso's (opposite) situation on the River Tweed makes the ancient Border town popular with anglers.

Smailholm Tower: one of the most complete 16th-century tower houses. Their defensive style recalls the Borders' turbulent past.

The Lammermuir Hills (opposite), a natural frontier between Lothian and the Borders and the setting of Scott's novel The Bride of Lammermuir.

Lowland Discoveries

SOUTHWESTERN SCOTLAND

The Glasgow conurbation – once the powerhouse of heavy industry, now the epicentre of the post-industrial economy – is the metropolitan hub of Southwest Scotland, with its urban sprawl concentrated in and around the lower Clyde. But much of the region is rural and some of it is wild, even if it lacks the grandeur of the Highlands. Between the wide estuaries of Clyde and Solway you can, in fact, find a scaled-down version of modern Scotland: a great city rich in history, architecture and contemporary style, ports and holiday resorts on the Ayrshire coast, upland farms in south Lanarkshire, pretty villages and lonely hills in Dumfries and Galloway.

Ayrshire has a tourist industry driven by Robert Burns and his Alloway birthplace is a sacred place of pilgrimage for devotees. But it has other assets, including Turnberry with its Open Championship golf course and Culzean Castle, a magnificent, clifftop "family home" designed by the Georgian period's most distinguished architect, Robert Adam. It and its country park are now owned by the National Trust for Scotland, one of their few properties always in profit, and it attracts transatlantic visitors for the Eisenhower Presentation – the story of how General Eisenhower, who got to know the castle during World War Two, was given the use of one of its apartments for life.

North of Ayr is a string of ports and ferry terminals before the Clyde estuary retreats into the sheltered waters of the river's much reduced shipbuilding industry. Glasgow – once the second city of the British Empire for the ships, locomotives, bridges and steel it sent round the world – is on their doorstep; a city which has shaken off its grimy image and re-invented itself as one of the most popular business and leisure destinations in Europe.

Where Edinburgh looked to the East and the European mainland Glasgow looked to the West and the Americas. As it transformed itself from quiet-living cathedral, university and market town into industrial behemoth – a process which happened so fast it has been called an "instant city" – it first built its fortune on trade. The Clyde became the gateway to the West Indies and the Eastern seaboard of America and

Glasgow Science Centre and the much loved paddle steamer Waverley. The River Clyde, once the cradle of a global shipbuilding industry, is still important to Glasgow's post-industrial transformation.

the 18th-century writer Daniel Defoe was able to describe Glasgow as "the cleanest and beautifullest and best built city in Britain." Its wealthy "tobacco barons" swept aside most of the city's medieval past and commissioned some of its finest architecture. Traces of their trade remain in the street names – Virginia Street, Jamaica Street – of what is now known as the Merchant City.

With the coming of the Industrial Revolution the city's population exploded. The Glasgow of dismal working class tenements, triumphant civic and commercial buildings and self-important suburbs came into being. Much of the best remains. The Victorian city centre is built on a grid; its urban motorways fly and swoop, its streets buzz with energy and its people are famous for warm hearts and mordant wit. Modern Glasgow has re-deployed its historical talent for innovation and enterprise. Its fashion stores are among the best in the country, its cultural life is vigorous and much of its new architecture is cutting edge.

Glasgow's suburbs spill into Lanarkshire along the valley of the Clyde, an iconic river modest in width but mighty in influence. It powered the textile mills of the Industrial Revolution (the explorer-missionary David Livingstone was born in Blantyre, one of its mill villages) and it waters the orchards and meadows of fruit growers and farmers. Lanark, an ancient town with strong associations with William Wallace,

Scotland's famous "freedom fighter", has an important livestock market, and below the town, in a wooded gorge noisy with the Falls of Clyde, is New Lanark, living museum, social experiment and World Heritage Site. In the early 18th century it became Britain's first "model village", where mill owners and philanthropists David Dale and Robert Owen provided decent housing, free schooling and other welfare benefits for employees and their children.

South of Lanark the Clyde rises in shapely uplands on the edge of Dumfries and Galloway – a great swathe of haunting, history-rich countryside and coast often by-passed by visitors heading north from the Border. (They might just pause at Gretna Green, which was the first available community where eloping couples from England could take advantage of Scotland's different marriage laws).

Dumfries, the "Queen of the South", is the only town of any size in the region. It has a splendid site on the River Nith, and although much of its historic character has been lost to piecemeal development, the red sandstone centre and handsome riverfront are full of interest. Robert Burns farmed at nearby Ellisland and lived and died in a house in Mill Vennel. Both are now museums. But the town's greatest asset is a hinterland of quiet, pastoral loveliness and its proximity to the Solway coast, where you can find some of the most charming small towns and villages in Scotland.

Sunset on Turnberry Lighthouse. This Ayrshire landmark has been familiar to generations of golfers, including stars of the international circuit, who have played Turnberry's Open Championship course.

Bedroom, The Mackintosh House, Hunterian Art Gallery, Glasgow

Drawing Room Lamp and Wall Stencils, The Hill House, Helensburgh

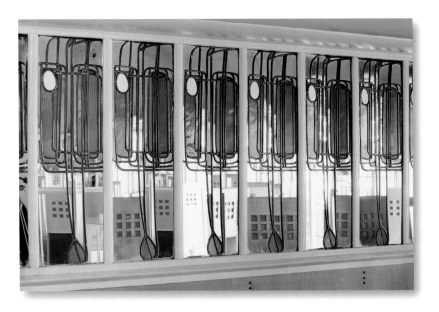

Wall Decoration, Room de Luxe, Willow Tea Rooms, Glasgow

Detail of South Face, House for an Art Lover, Glasgow

Charles Rennie Mackintosh

The man who most comprehensively represents Glasgow's flair for innovative design is Charles Rennie Mackintosh, whose international stature in the European Art Nouveau movement and pantheon of ground-breaking architects has steadily grown since his death in 1928. "Toshie", or CRM, was the city's Renaissance man – architect, interior designer and painter – and the most significant member of a quartet of young designers known as "the Four". In their search for a distinctive modern voice they collaborated on designs for furniture, metalwork and illustrations known as the Glasgow Style.

Mackintosh went on to design some of the city's most fascinating buildings, and his legacy has bred many contemporary imitators, whose output of jewellery and furniture labours under the soubriquet Mockintosh. If you find yourself sitting on a dining chair with a back like an upright ladder, that's Mockintosh. The real CRM, the fourth of 11 children, was born in the modest district of Townshead, near Glasgow Cathedral, in 1865. When he was 16 he was apprenticed first to Glasgow architect John Hutchison and then to the firm of Honeyman and Keppie, where he did his major work.

A fellow apprentice was Herbert McNair and together they attended evening classes at art school where they met two student sisters, Margaret and Frances Macdonald, whom they were each to marry. All four brought their own creativity to their collaborations, but CRM's voice was the most original. He had a masterly grasp of light, shade and space, and his work was informed by a blend of Scottish romantic traditions, Art Nouveau and the simplicity of Japanese forms.

His first important building, in 1893, was the *Glasgow Herald* offices in Mitchell Street. Now called The Lighthouse, this building fittingly became Scotland's Centre for Design, Architecture and the City in 1999, when Glasgow had the status of UK City of Architecture and Design. In 1900 he married Margaret Macdonald and in 1903 became a partner in Honeyman and Keppie, designing a run of landmark buildings: Scotland Street School, the Willow Tearoom in Sauchiehall Street (commissioned by his most enthusiastic patron, Miss Kate Cranston) and his magnum opus, Glasgow School of Art. They were to turn him into a cult figure of the European avant-garde.

Mackintosh believed in the total integration of his designs, inside and out, and commanded every detail. He was not an easy client. When he parted from Honeyman and Keppie in 1913 to set up his own business he failed to secure enough commissions, and in some disillusionment he and Margaret left Glasgow, moving first to Suffolk and then to London. (The popular version of their departure is that a "philistine" city rejected its most talented son, but Glasgow's economy was in trouble and there was little cash for avant-garde architecture).

He began to concentrate on watercolours and textile design, and to stretch their income they left London in 1923 for Port Vendres in the South of France, where Mackintosh produced some of his most eloquent landscape paintings. Five years later they returned, Mackintosh gravely ill with throat cancer. He died in London aged 60.

His achievements as an architect spanned only about 13 years, but during that period his opus of public buildings, commercial premises, churches and private homes anticipated the European modernists and made an enduring impact on the city of his birth. As well as the completed buildings he left dozens of designs which were never executed; although one – the House for an Art Lover – was finally built over several years and opened to the public in 1996.

For obvious reasons the innovative Clyde Auditorium, part of the Scottish Exhibition and Conference Centre in Glasgow, is nicknamed the Armadillo.

The majestic Kelvingrove Art Gallery and Museum, in the west end of Glasgow, is a monument to Victorian aspiration and one of the most visited cultural centres in Scotland.

"Auld Ayr, wham ne'er a town surpasses, For honest men and bonny lasses" – as Robert Burns described the Ayrshire capital in his comic narrative poem, Tam o' Shanter (1791).

Robert Burns

"A man's a man for a' that". No one better exemplifies his own words than Burns himself, genius of the romantic lyric, master of the comic satire, global celebrity to the Scots diaspora, and flawed human being; the left-leaning Scottish nationalist and inspiration of liberals and socialists who once contemplated taking a job on a Jamaican slave plantation, became an active Freemason, and ended his life as an exciseman – a loyal functionary of the British state. There are so many contradictions in the life and personality of Scotland's "national poet" that it has been easier to sentimentalise him and turn him into a cult. Even within his own short lifetime the Edinburgh literati chose to present him as an unlettered son of the soil whose talent was almost mystical. "The heaven-taught ploughman," they called him, ignoring the fact that he knew Latin and French, had a self-evident mastery of English grammar and had been sent to private tutors by his tenant farmer father.

Robert Burns was born in 1759 on January 25th – the date annually celebrated by the ritual of the Burns Supper. His birthplace in Alloway, now the Burns Cottage Museum, was built by his father, but the family moved several times before settling in Mauchline, where he met Jean Armour. Burns started writing verses when he was still in his teens, and he fathered the first of several illegitimate children as he courted Jean Armour, a romance which led to a troubled marriage and nine children, only three of whom survived infancy.

The poet wrote in English as well as Scots, and his lightness of touch with Scots dialect has made his work

The Globe Inn, much patronised by Burns.

internationally available. He was a harbinger of the Romantic Movement and a strong influence on the English poets Wordsworth, Coleridge and Shelley, as well as the young Walter Scott, who met him in Edinburgh when Scott was 16. Burns was invited to the capital after the Kilmarnock publication of his first volume in 1786. It included some of his best-known poems – *The Cotter's Saturday Night*, *The Twa Dogs*, *To a Mouse* – and was an instant sensation. He was greeted enthusiastically by Edinburgh's men of letters and entertained by its beau monde, and began an intense relationship with Agnes "Nancy" McLehose, the "Clarinda" of their letters. But she was not easily seduced, so Burns turned his attention to her servant, who bore him a son.

His marriage to Jean Armour had faltered over his passion for Mary Campbell – Highland Mary – but when he left Edinburgh in 1788 he returned to Jean and they moved to the farm of Ellisland, near Dumfries. When the farm failed he was employed by Customs and Excise in Dumfries, where he wrote much of his most memorable poetry, including *Tam-o'-Shanter*, *Auld Lang Syne* and the lyrics for over 100 traditional Scots melodies. His health was never strong; his heart was weakened by rheumatic fever, but it was an acute infection after a tooth extraction that led to his death when he was only 37.

Few argue that he had genius, but the 20th-century poet and Scottish nationalist Hugh MacDiarmid tilted against the cult of Burns, believing the iconography and the ritualised silliness of the Burns Supper trivialised Burns's achievements and did Scotland little good.

The Ayrshire town of Girvan was first an important fishing port and then a popular resort for Glaswegians, especially "day trippers."
Culzean Castle (opposite): this magnificent Robert Adam building on the Ayrshire cliffs is now owned by the National Trust for Scotland.

The Southern Uplands near Moffat: these lonely Border hills sustain many of Scotland's sheep farms and offer fine walking.
The first Duke of Queensberry built Drumlanrig Castle in the 17th century (opposite), a graceful Renaissance style palace of pink sandstone in the Dalveen Pass.

Dryburgh Abbey: the pastoral setting of this 12th-century ruin adds much to its charm. Despite burnings by English troops it flourished in the 15th century.
The moat, towers and battlements of the medieval Caerlaverock Castle (opposite) reflects its turbulent history near the English border.

Riches of the Middle Ground

CENTRAL SCOTLAND

Above the narrow waist of Scotland there is an abrupt transition from Lowlands to Highlands. Travellers between Edinburgh and Glasgow can see for themselves the wall of hills which rises from the flatlands of the Forth basin and marks the Highland Boundary Line – the geological fault which crosses the country coast-to-coast from Helensburgh in the west to Stonehaven in the east. North of Glasgow are the hills of Loch Lomond and the Trossachs, with a scatter of mountains above 3000 ft; north of Edinburgh are the outriders of the Perthshire ranges, which include some of Scotland's most popular peaks for hillwalkers. And to the east of this middle ground is an anomaly: the Kingdom of Fife.

The kingdom no longer has a king but its principal town, Dunfermline, was the capital of Scotland for 600 years and its fine abbey church, which dates back to the 12th century, is the burial place of several early monarchs. Dunfermline was also the birthplace of the Scots-American philanthropist Andrew Carnegie, who endowed his native town with public buildings, and whose life is recalled in the Andrew Carnegie Birthplace Museum. To the east, Fife thrusts itself into the North Sea between the Forth and Tay estuaries and has tenaciously retained its ancient title, although it also has claim to a more recent one: the kingdom of golf.

Often windswept but always graceful, the university town of St Andrews is the famous home of the Old Course, and the Royal and Ancient Golf Club. On its coastal site near Fife Ness, St Andrews became a place of pilgrimage in the 8th century, although legend has it that the ship bearing the relics of the apostle Andrew was shipwrecked on the coast four centuries earlier. By the beginning of the 10th century the town had the pre-eminent priory and bishopric in Scotland, and its cathedral – now a picturesque ruin – was consecrated in 1318 in the presence of Robert the Bruce. The university, the oldest in Scotland, was founded in 1412, but as a redoubt of the Catholic Church St Andrews became a place of martyrdom during the Protestant Reformation. Three Reformation martyrs were burned at the stake, events commemorated by the Martyrs' Monument on the green near the sea.

Loch Achray, Queen Elizabeth Forest Park. The hills and lochs of the Trossachs – a name which simply means "bristly country" – make Highland glamour available to Scotland's Lowland population centres.

The hub of central Scotland is the royal burgh of Stirling, dominated by a spectacular building and viewpoint: Stirling Castle, which crowns a 250-ft volcanic plug, is every bit as impressive as Edinburgh Rock. This natural fortress made Stirling significant from the 12th century onwards, and the town had its most turbulent moments during Scotland's Wars of Independence against the English, when first the Battle of Stirling Bridge and then the Battle of Bannockburn confirmed the reputations of the great warrior patriots William Wallace and Robert the Bruce. An extravagant monument to Wallace, raised by the Victorians in Gothic style, stands on nearby Abbey Craig.

From there the leaping ramparts of the Trossachs and Perthshire seem almost close enough to touch. Not for nothing is Stirling called "the gateway to the Highlands". Loch Lomond, which has become something of a playground for the Glasgow conurbation, is on its doorstep, and the gorgeous hill roads of the Trossachs – a name which simply means "bristly country" – link the smaller lochs of Achray and Katrine. This area, a microcosm of the grander Highlands to the north, was an inspiration to the Romantic poets. Sir Walter Scott's ballad *The Lady of the Lake* refers to Loch Katrine, and there are strong associations with Rob Roy MacGregor, the most famous scion of the MacGregor clan. He is buried at Balquidder, near the town of Callander.

Landlocked Perthshire is arguably the most beautiful region of Scotland, not so much for its high peaks and managed wilderness, but for the civilising influence of its rural economy: its rich broadleaf woodlands, pastoral glens, salmon rivers and handsome towns and villages. If it had a coast it would be perfect, although the long glacial lochs of Loch Tay, Loch Rannoch and Lochearn provide something of the drama of the sea and many of the same leisure activities. The River Tay, Scotland's longest, debouches from its loch at Kenmore and makes its way through the cathedral town of Dunkeld to the city of Perth – yet another capital of medieval Scotland.

Perth calls itself the "Fair City" and lies in a bowl of wooded hills on the interface between Highlands and Lowlands. North of the Tay, which gains in girth as it travels through Perth towards its estuary, is Scone Palace, the ancestral seat of the earls of Mansfield. The name of Scone resonates powerfully with all patriotic Scots. Between the 9th and 13th centuries its abbey was the custodian of the Stone of Destiny, on which Scottish monarchs were crowned until it was purloined in 1296 by England's Edward I, "Hammer of the Scots", and installed in the Coronation throne in Westminster Abbey. It remained in the base of the wooden throne until 1950, when it was "stolen" again and, after many adventures, recovered and reclaimed by Westminster Abbey. There it stayed until 1996, when 700 years after the original theft it was finally and ceremonially returned to Scotland. It now rests in Edinburgh Castle.

Loch Katrine, the most popular stretch of water in the Trossachs, does double duty as beauty spot and reservoir. Since 1859 it has been supplying most of Glasgow's water.

The National Wallace Monument – a Victorian initiative – honours the Scottish patriot William Wallace and his 1297 victory at Stirling Bridge.
Not for nothing is Stirling called "gateway to the Highlands." Its dramatic castle (opposite) occupies a strategic crag near the River Forth.

Dusk on Loch Arklet; a popular beauty spot in the Loch Lomond and the Trossachs National Park.

Loch Lomond, with Ben Lomond (opposite) on the east shore. At 973 m it is the most southerly of Scotland's "Munros" – mountains over 3000 ft.

It's still possible to travel on steam trains on some of Scotland's scenic railways. This route is through Auch Glen, near Tyndrum.
Perhaps Scotland's most unusual visitor attraction, the Falkirk Wheel (opposite) lifts boats between the Forth and Clyde and the Union canals.

Pittenweem. The charming old fishing villages of the East Neuk of Fife command the wide entrance to the Firth of Forth.
Graceful St Andrews (opposite), home of Scotland's oldest university and most celebrated golf course. In the foreground are the cathedral ruins.

The Royal and Ancient Clubhouse, Old Course, St Andrews

Gleneagles, Perthshire

Carnoustie, Angus

Turnberry, Ayrshire

Scottish Golf

Who first hit a stone into a rabbit hole with a stick on the grassy dunes of the North Sea coast? The Dutch and Scots both have claims on the origins of golf, as both countries can produce historical references to some kind of golf-like game played by shepherds and sailors. But these rudimentary efforts were mere ancestors of the modern game, which beyond argument began in Scotland, which had the earliest permanent golf courses, devised the written rules and led the way to the 18-hole course which has become the international standard.

There is continued debate in Scotland about which golf course is the oldest. One account of the first recorded game of golf in the archives of the Royal Burgess Golfing Society, a venerable club which numbers Jack Nicklaus among its members, claims golf was played in Edinburgh in 1456 on Bruntsfield Links, which 300 years later became the club's home. Bruntsfield Links remain, no longer a golf course, and the Royal Burgess's premises are now in the suburb of Barnton.

Golf has been played on the links of St Andrews for many centuries, and the Royal and Ancient Golf Club of St Andrews, which established the 18-hole course, remains the international ruling arbiter on the game. The Club plays on the world-famous Old Course. Some claim Edinburgh has the oldest playing golf course: Musselburgh Old Links Golf Course, on the Forth littoral, which like many of Scotland's most prestigious courses, including the Old Course at St Andrews, is a public one. Records show that golf has been played there since 1672, although it's said that Mary Queen of Scots enjoyed a round on the links in 1567.

Musselburgh is also a former home of the world's oldest club, the Honourable Company of Edinburgh Golfers, which was founded in 1744 and first began playing on Leith Links. As its membership grew so did its self-importance, and in 1891 it moved down the East Lothian coast to the village of Gullane and turned itself into a private club, today generally reckoned the UK's most elite, with the beautiful links course of Muirfield. If you approach the formidable iron gates which protect the entrance to its opulent clubhouse you soon discover how jealously Muirfield defends its privileges. It's said that some members may even resent the disruption caused by the Open Championship, held there every few years in rotation with four English clubs and four other Scottish ones: Carnoustie, Royal Troon, Turnberry and St Andrews.

Like the Royal and Ancient, which was founded ten years later in 1754 by 22 "local noblemen and gentlemen being admirers of the ancient and healthful exercise of golf", Muirfield does not admit women as members. There was, however, one radical development at the R and A in 2007, when the Old Course staged the British Women's Open for the first time and the competitors were graciously allowed to use the facilities of the clubhouse.

For all the entrenched attitudes of these two ancient clubs the Scottish game has always been a democratic one, perhaps because of its humble origins among the bored shepherds and idle sailors who knocked around stones on the foreshores which became Scotland's supreme links courses. It is the nation's most popular participating sport and the public courses are open to anyone, from plumbers to princes, who can afford the green fees.

In a game which is now global, Scotland still has the greatest number of golf courses in the world in relation to its population; over 500, with more at the design stage. With complete confidence it can continue to call itself the home of golf.

"The Fair City of Perth": the town's situation defines its soubriquet. It rests in a bowl of hills on the River Tay.
RRS Discovery (opposite), the exploration ship of Scott of the Antarctic, is now a waterfront attraction in its home port of Dundee.

You can't miss Blair Castle. The palatial whitewashed seat of the Dukes of Atholl overlooks the main road route north, beyond Pitlochry.
Loch Tay (opposite), bears the remains of 23 prehistoric island settlements called crannogs – unique dwellings built above the water on wooden platforms.

A Tangle of Islands

ARGYLL & THE ISLES

There are some 780 major islands off the Scottish coast, not to mention the minor ones no one has bothered to count. Most of the scattered pieces of this jigsaw lie off the western seaboard, and many millennia ago the seaboard itself was fractured and riven by the titanic forces of fire and ice. Together, the Hebridean islands and west coast are among the most complex geographical arrangements in Europe, and Scotland's most distinctive physical feature. They also offer its most hauntingly beautiful seascapes.

The great Firth of Clyde is the southern frontier of this tangle of land and water, which has so many natural harbours it became both haven and target for every passing seafarer, notably the Irish and the Vikings. The tip of the Kintyre peninsula is only 12 miles from the north coast of Ireland, and it's said that St Columba first set foot in Scotland near the Mull of Kintyre. When Gaelic speakers arrived in Argyll from Ireland they established an early kingdom, Dalriada, between AD 500 and 800. Its most conspicuous relic is Dunadd Fort, windswept earthworks on the Argyll coast.

The region remains a challenge for maritime traffic of all kinds, including the ferries which serve a network of routes. The well-populated Clyde islands of Arran and Bute are reached from the Cowal peninsula and the estuary ports. Jura and Islay have ferry links with Kintyre and Oban, while Mull, Iona, Coll, Tiree and Colonsay are also reached from this Argyll railhead and resort, which is the main seaway to the Hebrides.

Oban is a town, not a city, but on the rural seaboard of the West Highlands it almost feels like a metropolis. Its nature is a mixture of old and new, charm and functionalism, but its setting is incomparable. The island of Kerrera is flung across Oban Bay like a stepping stone to the sharp peaks of Mull. Island-hopping begins here, on one of the largest of the Inner Hebrides with the prettiest port: Tobermory, with tall, brightly painted houses fronting its harbour. Mull has a respectable mountain, 3000 ft Ben More, dramatic 13th-century Duart Castle, seat of the MacLeans, and some spectacular shorelines. It's also

Scotland's medieval castles, often in spectacular sites, make irresistible photographic targets. This is Castle Stalker in Appin, north of Oban. It was built around 1540 and restored in the 1960s.

the through-route to Iona – a low-lying Arcadia of sheep-cropped turf and sugar-white beaches.

There are few places to stay overnight on the tiny island of Iona. Many of its visitors are pilgrims come to honour the place where, in the 6th century, St Columba arrived from Ireland to set up the community that turned Iona into the Christian centre of Europe. In their sights is the squat profile of Iona Abbey, abandoned during the Reformation but restored in the 1930s by the new Iona Community. In its ancient cemetery are the graves of almost 50 clan chiefs, Lords of the Isles and European kings, but few are identifiable.

From Mull you can also reach the sister islands of Coll and Tiree, most distant of the Inner Hebrides. Tiree's Gaelic name, *Tir fo Thuinn*, means "land below the waves". It has only two hills, both no higher than 400 ft, and a reputation for sunshine and strong winds which have made it popular with windsurfers and surfers. Coll is only slightly less low-lying, and like delightful Colonsay to the south they are crofting islands whose summer populations are swelled by holidaymakers.

Each Hebridean island has its own character – some lofty, some flat, some green and welcoming with bays of dazzling sand, some bleak and inhospitable with rocky foreshores and drab peat bogs. But along with much of the neighbouring mainland they all belong to the *Gaedhealchd*, that part of Scotland where the language and culture of the Gaels, who

migrated from Ireland probably around the 5th century, have survived, and where many of the indigenous people (often outnumbered by incomers these days) are bilingual. In a resurgence of pride in Gaelic, which before the 11th century was spoken by a large part of Scotland, the language has been restored to road signs and public buildings.

The most southern of the Inner Hebrides are Islay and Jura, such close neighbours that from Kintyre they look like one island. But they are very different. Jura has three impressive mountains called the Paps of Jura, and few people. It has some literary celebrity as the place where George Orwell wrote *1984*, while more populous Islay's claims to fame are both ancient and modern. Between the 12th and 16th centuries Islay was the seat of power of the Clan Donald, who wrested the Atlantic seaboard from Norse colonists. MacDonald chiefs held the title Lord of the Isles and controlled the west from Kintyre to Lewis. Relics of their palace and parliament, Finlaggan, remain on two islets on Loch Finlaggan, where the Lords convened their own form of government and met Scottish, English and European monarchs on equal terms.

Today, Islay is the kingdom of island malts. It has no fewer than eight malt whisky distilleries. Famous for their peaty flavour, classics include Laphroaig, Lagavulin, Ardbeg and Caol Ila.

The shell beaches of Iona are famous for their white sand, aquamarine shallows and heartlifting views. Some claim their tranquillity carries the spiritual legacy which St Columba bequeathed the island.

The lighthouse on the island of Lismore, at the mouth of Loch Linnhe. Grouped behind on the mainland are the Glencoe mountains. Wintry skies over Mull (opposite), one of the largest of the Inner Hebrides. Its highest mountain is Ben More, 966 m.

Duart Castle, at the entrance to the Sound of Mull, is home to the chiefs of the Macleans of Duart.

Ancient Monarchs of Scotland

Kenneth MacAlpine is the man who is called the first King of Scotland, then known by its Roman name, Alba, although the Kingdom of Alba was missing some large and important bits of the country we know today. A consummate power broker, MacAlpine's ancestors came from Antrim in Ireland, heartland of a Gaelic tribe called the Scotti, who crossed the Irish Sea and settled on the Argyll coast around AD 500 and founded the Kingdom of Dalriada. Scotland's origins as a sovereign nation began on a lumpy hummock of turf, heather and peat bog in Argyll, which is all that remains of Dalriada's pomp today.

First the Scotti had to come to some kind of accommodation with the Picts, who had seen off the Romans to the point where the masters of the civilised world were obliged to retreat from North Britain, throwing up two coast-to-coast barricades behind them: Hadrian's Wall and Antonine's Wall. The fiery Picts were also of Celtic ancestry, and throughout the Dark Ages both the newly arrived Gaels and long-established Picts had to confront the Vikings, who made serious efforts to colonise Scotland. In AD 843, Scots and Picts united under MacAlpine and in time both peoples merged into one.

But not before they had dealt with the Angles, who also made a genetic contribution to the Scottish mix. They were Teutonic immigrants from Northumbria who controlled the Lothians and the south, including Edinburgh. The future capital didn't become part of the new kingdom until AD 962. Internecine feuds were fierce over the next century as different factions and families struggled for power.

During this period, according to Shakespeare, the tyrant Macbeth murdered his rival Duncan. But what is known of Macbeth tells a different story. He was born in 1005 and both he and Duncan, grandsons of King Malcolm II, had legitimate claims on the Scottish throne. Duncan's rule was characterised by six savage years of expansionist warfare, and when he died in battle in 1040 his cousin Macbeth was then crowned. During his 17-year reign Macbeth was considered a benevolent and progressive ruler, and when he died in 1057 Duncan's son succeeded him: Malcolm III, known as Malcolm Canmore.

At this time the Northern Isles and much of the west coast were occupied by Scandinavia, but Malcolm was prepared to tolerate this rather than waste resources evicting the Vikings. The most influential thing he did was to marry Margaret, niece of the Anglo-Saxon king Edward the Confessor, and thus bring royal blood from England into the dynastic line. Queen Margaret, Scotland's only saint, was a woman of great and practical piety who was canonised for her services to the poor and fidelity to the church. Malcolm and Margaret built the palace, abbey and monastery of Dunfermline, which for several centuries became intimately associated with the births, lives, and burials of Scotland's royalty. Their son, David I, founded the 12th-century Border abbeys and is the man credited with consolidating Scotland's nationhood through the establishment of burghs.

This dynasty persisted until the late 13th century and the two "interregnums" when Scotland lost its sovereignty and came under English rule. But not for long. There followed the Wars of Independence and the "puppet" kingship of John Balliol, a descendant of David I, before another of David's descendants came to the fore to unite the warring Scots nobles against their English overlords. His name was Robert the Bruce.

The rest, you might say, is history. Bruce was a founder member of the Stuart dynasty, and Scotland was never again without its own monarch until 1606, when James VI, son of Mary Queen of Scots, succeeded Elizabeth I of England and, through the Union of the Crowns, became king of both nations.

This seafood kiosk on the Oban waterfront does brisk business with visitors to the resort and island ferry terminal.
Marine congestion at the South Pier in Oban Bay (opposite). On the skyline is McCaig's Tower, the town's most distinctive landmark.

Machrie Moor on the Isle of Arran is rich in prehistoric sites, including burial chambers and at least six stone circles.
The Kyles of Bute (opposite), between the island of Bute and the Cowal peninsula, is a challenge for Clyde estuary mariners.

Jura's shapely mountains are known as the Paps of Jura. Among the larger of the Inner Hebrides, it is the least populated.
Port Ellen (opposite) is the capital of Islay, The most southerly of the Inner Hebrides, Islay is home to eight malt whisky distilleries.

The seat of the Dukes of Argyll, chiefs of Clan Campbell, is Inveraray Castle on Loch Fyne. Completed in 1789, it is still their family home. Glen Kinglas from Loch Fyne (opposite), the longest of the deep sea lochs which bite their way into the mainland from the Firth of Clyde.

The multi-coloured harbour houses of Tobermory, capital of Mull, break with the tradition of whitewash commonly found on Highland waterfronts. Moody weather brings all the colours of the rainbow to Scallastle Bay (opposite) on the Isle of Mull.

Iona Abbey: the medieval building replaced St Columba's monastery, founded in AD 563, and is a burial place of Scottish kings.

The Celtic Influence

Little is known about Scotland before 4000 BC. Its earliest people were nameless hunters and fisherman whose Neolithic relics – standing stones, burial chambers and settlements – continue to intrigue archaeologists. It isn't until after the westward migrations of the Celtic tribes, driven by their enemies to the edge of Europe, and the arrival of the Romans, that reliable records begin.

When the Romans first arrived in Britain in 55 BC the object of their general, Julius Caesar, was the subjugation of its Celtic tribes, who gave refuge and support to their rebellious kin across the Channel in Roman Gaul. During the 400 years of Roman occupation the invaders found three peoples who were fundamentally Celtic: the Britons in England, the Scotti in Ireland and the Picts in Scotland. The Picts, who lived north of the Forth and Clyde valleys, were a confederation of tribes descended from the Caledonii – a name which survives today in all things Caledonian. They were never assimilated by the Romans.

The Celts were not a single people but an aggregate of tribes loosely linked by language, religion and culture, and often just as eager to fight each other as Romans. They are believed to have migrated into Europe from Asia Minor, and were the dominant people in central and northern Europe from the early Iron Age onwards. By 700 BC they had also become powerful in Iberia. They began to infiltrate the British Isles between 500 and 100 BC, bringing

The Kildalton Cross, on Islay

with them their skill in working iron and "importing" the first iron plough. They were our first farmers, living in timber houses with thatched roofs in large extended families, early versions of the clans which persisted in the Highlands. Creative as well as combative, they practised a polytheistic form of religion; their priests were the Druids and their shrines were hilltops, groves and lakes.

They built a huge number of hill forts and were no pushover for the great Roman war machine. In Britain one of their (temporarily) most successful generals was Queen Boudicca, or Boadicea, whose warrior nature and leadership qualities were no exception in Celtic society, where women had equal status, could own property and choose their own husbands. But as the Romans tightened their grip on what is now England and more and more of its colonised people inter-married and became Romanised, Celtic culture declined, to survive most strongly in Ireland, Wales and Scotland.

They were an artistic people, expert in metalwork and stone-carving; the most familiar example of Celtic art is the Celtic cross, its distinctive geometric design reproduced down the centuries in jewellery, tombstones and monuments. They had a written language, although few manuscripts survive (the most celebrated is Ireland's illustrated Book of Kells) and a vigorous oral tradition, best conserved in the ballads and narratives of the *Gaedhealachd*. In Scotland the Picts were masters of stone-carving; the Scotti brought their own genre of Celtic traditions from Ireland, and that which we call Gaelic culture today owes much to both.

Summer cruises on Loch Etive are the best way to see its eloquent waters and the Argyll mountains which surround it.
Kilchurn Castle (opposite), at the north end of Loch Awe, is one of Scotland's most romantic ruins and a former Campbell stronghold.

Fertile Fields and Fairytale Castles

THE NORTHEAST

Between the firths of Tay and Moray a great shoulder of land juts into the North Sea, with a character and past very different from the rest of Scotland. This eastern seaboard and its hinterland are largely agricultural; the exceptions are the cities of Dundee and Aberdeen. But the fertile croplands of Angus and the famous beef farms of Aberdeenshire have been hard won. "Our ancestors imposed their will on Buchan," observed the northeast writer John R. Allan, describing its flintiest corner, "…at great expense of labour and endurance, of weariness and suffering."

There was a time when the *Gaedhealechd* reached into these parts, and there are wild echoes of Highland desolation in the Grampian uplands of Angus or the outriders of the Cairngorms, which push into Aberdeenshire. But more than anything this is a managed landscape, shaped to the scale of human endeavour, and for the visitor its loveliness is versatile and subtle. It was also once a stronghold of the Picts, while many centuries later came the noble families and wealthy merchants who raised some of Britain's most handsome fortified homes.

The sea has played a huge role in the history of the energetic Northeast, and still does. Trade, fish and oil have been the drivers of its prosperity. Aberdeen, whose fortunes rose on trade with the Baltic ports and its hub markets for fish and farming, became a major player in the North Sea oil industry 30 years ago. The Granite City takes its soubriquet from the ubiquitous building material of its architecture, has a 6th-century cathedral and the second oldest university in the country, and has always been a place of stout self-confidence, aloof from the rest of urban Scotland.

Dundee, on the Tay estuary, also has a long maritime history. It was once Scotland's leading importer of French claret, then the home port of a large whaling fleet, then the city which built an economy on jute, importing the raw material of its textile industry from the Indian sub-continent. Today it has put its old docks to work in the tourist industry. R.R.S.

Standing on its own giant rock near Stonehaven, gaunt Dunottar Castle provides clifftop spectacle. During the 17th century the Scottish crown jewels were concealed from Cromwell's roundheads in the castle.

Discovery, the ship which carried Captain Scott's expedition to the Antarctic, has returned to the city where it was built, and is now the centrepiece of waterfront attractions. More significantly, Dundee and its university have become world leaders in research into medicine and life sciences.

The city's hinterland is the fertile county of Angus, an eloquent fusion of hill, glen, farmland, beaches and cliffs. It has Pictish sculptured stones, a surviving Celtic round tower and Arbroath Abbey, now an elegant ruin, which witnessed a key event in Scottish history: the Declaration of Arbroath, when in 1320 the Scottish nobles reaffirmed their determination to maintain the independence of their country. Angus's most interesting towns include Montrose, built at the mouth of a vast tidal basin, and Forfar, gateway to the childhood homes of two famous people: J.M Barrie, author of *Peter Pan*, who was born in Kirriemuir, and Elizabeth Bowes-Lyon, the late Queen Mother, who spent her early life in glorious Glamis Castle.

The Scottish heartland of Britain's Royal family is, however, Aberdeenshire, where the lovely valley of the River Dee became "Royal Deeside" in the 19th century, when Queen Victoria fell in love with its Highland character. Her husband, Prince Albert, acquired the Balmoral estate in 1852 and built Balmoral Castle, a Victorian Gothic extravagance. It has been a royal residence ever since; the present Queen and her family spend part of the summer at Balmoral, attend church in the nearby hamlet of Crathie, and do their shopping – after a fashion – in the little town of Ballater; all of which has created its own tourist industry, although the upper Dee valley is well worth exploring for its own sake.

The Eastern Highlands crowd round the village of Braemar, site of the country's most prestigious Highland Gathering (it's always attended by the Royal holidaymakers) before the graceful Dee loses the hills as it spreads towards Aberdeen and the sea. As the Northeast coast runs along boiling cliffs and rocky bays, with austere fishing villages and ports clinging to its edge like limpets, it seems a truculent seaboard, bordered by the "stony fields and diffident trees" of John R. Allan's hard-won land. But as Buchan yields to Moray the coast itself becomes more yielding; the cliffs become sands, the inland towns of Forres, Fochabers and Elgin have the softer character of golden sandstone and there is a growing sense that labour has time for reflection on the benevolent Moray Firth.

Here the spiritual community of Findhorn – famous internationally as the Findhorn Foundation – have turned sand dunes into flourishing vegetable gardens, and the town of Nairn, with beaches, hotels and golf links, is the premier resort of "the sunshine coast", which claims to have more hours of sunny weather than anywhere else on the mainland.

Always a major fishing and trading port, Aberdeen Harbour has never been busier since it began servicing the North Sea oil industry. Its activity seems to surge into the city centre.

Fraserburgh Harbour: this grey, sternly-forged fishing port is one of a chain which has made the truculent north-east coast productive. Crovie's houses (opposite) cling like limpets to the north-east cliffs. They are built gable-end to the sea better to resist its storms.

Once the Burnett family seat, Crathes Castle is a handsome example of the Aberdeenshire school of 16th-century tower houses.

Arbroath (opposite): home of the "smokie" – hot-smoked haddock – and the Declaration of Arbroath, which in 1320 affirmed Scotland's independence from England.

This lyrical landscape near Huntly was once hard-worked by Picts, who left their mark with hill forts and monumental carved stones.

The Picts

The Picts are a puzzle – but not such a mysterious one as once believed. Although they left only fragments of written language something of their history and culture was recorded by several sources from the late 6th century, including Adomnan, the biographer of St Columba. They also left behind solid relics of their period in the carved monoliths and crosses which scatter the Scottish landscape, although most of the finest examples are now in museums. And in early Pictish times they are popularly associated with the brochs, or circular stone towers, bequeathed to them from the Iron Age.

The origin of their name is unknown, but the Latin word "picti" means "painted or tattooed people", and it's always been part of their legend that they were heavily tattooed, although the carvings of Pictish warriors, nobles and hunters show little evidence of tattoos. What is known is that they lived mainly in eastern and northern Scotland from Roman times until the 10th century. There are Pictish sites from Easter Ross to Lanarkshire, and the remains of Pictish houses have been unearthed as far north as Orkney; but because the Romans, chief chroniclers of the age, never got as far as Orkney this is a recent discovery.

The early Iron Age inhabitants of Scotland probably contributed to the Pictish gene pool, along with the Celtic tribes who migrated from mainland Europe. By the time they became known to the Romans they had evolved, it's believed, from the Caledonii who proved so troublesome to the imperial legions that they withdrew behind the defensive walls of Hadrian and Antonine. The Caledonii's greatest war leader was Calgacus, whose qualities were recorded by the Roman historian Tacitus, who credited Calgacus with this famous assessment of the invaders' scorched earth policy: "They create a desert and call it peace."

"Pictland" or "Pictavia" was the territory of a confederation of tribes whose unity, it's believed, was a response to the expansionist ambitions of the Romans. Early Picts sailed up and down the coast of Roman Britain committing acts of piracy, but when not fighting Romans, Vikings or Angles the Pictish people were essentially farmers, living in small communities of roundhouses and timbered halls. They used watermills and kilns, kept sheep and pigs and grew cereal crops and vegetables, while cattle and horses were a sign of wealth. They also had time to craft ornamental metalwork and, of course, exercise their talent as stone-carvers. Pictish art is essentially Celtic art; there are only theories about the purpose of many of their monumental stones and the meaning of their more obscure symbols, but some carvings include Latin writing and, as the Picts became Gaelicised, Christian references.

The Picts were well entrenched as the dominant people in Scotland when the Scotti arrived in Argyll from Ireland around the 5th century, importing the new religion and the Gaelic language. Their Kingdom of Dalriada had its own dynasties and territories until the 9th century, when their ruler Kenneth MacAlpine negotiated a "merger" with the Picts and the two peoples became founder members of the Kingdom of Alba, later Scotia. By this time Pictish stones often took the shape of crosses, as Christianity was well established through the mission of St Columba and his Iona community.

Among the most distinctive monumental stones which remain in their original sites are the Aberlemno Serpent Stone, in the Angus village of Aberlemno, and the Craw Stone, a 6ft high monolith on a hill near Rhynie, in Aberdeenshire. The Craw Stone is carved with a salmon and a Pictish Beast – a creature which appears on many other stones and is sometimes called the Pictish Elephant or Pictish Dragon, as it looks like a hybrid of both. The most fanciful theory about its identity is that the Pictish Beast is a representation of the Loch Ness Monster.

Commissioned by Prince Albert, the consort of Queen Victoria, Balmoral Castle became the queen's favourite retreat and remains a royal residence today. Today's seasonal residents enjoy this view of "Royal Deeside" from Balmoral (opposite). On the skyline is the long ridge of Lochnagar.

Scottish Castles

There is no part of Scotland where you won't find a castle; or at the very least the remains of one. But the Northeast is king of castle country. Aberdeenshire alone has more castles per acre of land than any other area of the United Kingdom. Among its prime farmland and hill-and-heather sporting estates you find every defensive feature of the last 3000 years, from the earthworks of Pictish and Roman forts through the mottes and Baileys of the Middle Ages to the baronial fantasies of the Victorians.

Although the region was never in the front line of Scotland's endemic wars with England it had its share of English occupations and domestic feuding. And, of course, there was a time when every noble family was required to defend its fief. Huntly Castle is a good example. Stronghold of the powerful Gordons, its majestic remains are a lesson in castle architecture as they extended and adapted their family home over five centuries. Another splendid ruin is Kildrummy Castle in the quiet Donside hills, once the seat of the Jacobite Earls of Mar. When the Jacobite rising of 1715 failed it was "disarmed" and partly dismantled, but enough survived for Historic Scotland to claim it as the most complete 13th-century castle in Scotland.

Aberdeenshire's most admired school of castle-building, however, arrived not with conflict but prosperity. As the port city grew wealthy on trade with the Baltic countries, Aberdeen's merchants aspired to country homes. But in the late 16th and 17th centuries defence was still an issue – and so began the elegant age of the tower house; less bellicose than the fortresses of the Middle Ages with their ditches, battlements and armouries, but still capable of resisting aggression, with tall, smooth walls hard to climb and high windows hard to breach.

The style reached perfection with Craigievar Castle, which is virtually unchanged since it was completed in 1626 for William Forbes, Baltic merchant and brother of the bishop of Aberdeen. A slender tower in the rolling upland between Don and Dee it has smooth, biscuit-coloured walls crowned by turrets, cupolas and crowstep gables, and is now owned by the National Trust for Scotland.

Another tower house fit for Cinderellas is Crathes Castle, near the Deeside town of Banchory. Also now the property of NTS it was raised on land granted to the Burnett family by Robert the Bruce in 1323, although the castle wasn't built and occupied until 1595.

Horror stories, not fairytales, have associations with Slains Castle, a gaunt clifftop ruin near Cruden Bay, between Peterhead and Aberdeen. This 16th-century seat of the Earls of Erroll once hosted the Irish writer Bram Stoker, author of the novel *Dracula*. Stoker was a frequent visitor to the golf resort and in 1895, when the castle was still habitable, was invited to stay by the resident earl. When *Dracula* was published two years later the locals decided he must have been inspired by their grim fortress.

But the most spectacular coastal castle in the Northeast is Dunnottar, which is almost an island castle. Its 12th-century bones rise like some organic growth from a great crag in the sea near Stonehaven, south of Aberdeen, and are reached by a bridge of land between two cliffs. This castle played a thrilling part in a key event in Scottish history when, during the Cromwellian wars, the Scottish regalia were brought to Dunnottar for safekeeping. When their refuge was besieged in 1652 the crown was smuggled out in the apron of the wife of the local minister, while the sword and sceptre were liberated in a bundle of flax by her servant.

The regalia were hidden under the pulpit of Kinneff Church for eight years, until it was safe to return them to their rightful home in Edinburgh Castle.

Fyvie Castle, once a fortress of Alexander III, was reconstructed in 1599. It's now owned by the National Trust for Scotland.

The childhood home of the late Queen Mother, exquisite Glamis Castle, in Angus, is the seat of the Earls of Strathmore and Kinghorne. The Highland Fault line meets the sea at Stonehaven (opposite), a dignified little fishing port which re-invented itself as a holiday resort.

Myths, Mountains and Malts

THE CENTRAL HIGHLANDS

The Great Glen is a stupendous gash that almost severs the north of Scotland from the rest of the country. It was caused by the movement of tectonic plates during the Ice Age, and now forms a steep-sided trench filled with the waters of three lochs. One of them is Scotland's most famous: Loch Ness. To the northeast is the city of Inverness, capital of the Highlands; to the southeast are Strathspey and the wild Cairngorm Mountains. This desolate massif, which rises to 1309 metres at Ben Macdui, has the fragile eco-system of sub-Arctic tundra. It is also a busy haunt of skiers, climbers and hillwalkers and requires protection, so is now the centrepiece of the Cairngorms National Park.

You can sail along the diagonal Great Glen fault line from the Moray Firth to Loch Linnhe – effectively coast to coast. The North Sea and Atlantic Ocean are linked by lochs, rivers and the Caledonian Canal, but most nautical activity is concentrated on Loch Ness, guardian of the resident "monster", which enthusiastically drives its tourist industry. The scattered village of Drumnadrochit, on its northern bank, is the

place to go for Loch Ness Monster boat trips, exhibitions and souvenirs. Nearby is one of Scotland's most theatrically sited ruins: Urquhart Castle, which stands on a headland overlooking Urquhart Bay.

Loch Ness is the longest stretch of uninterrupted water for sailors navigating the Caledonian Canal, which is only truly a canal for about 35 km of the 96km-long waterway. Today it is a playground for pleasure craft. The small capacity of its 29 locks makes it virtually useless for modern commercial shipping, although the canal was built with the aim of sparing coastal vessels the hazardous passage round the north coast of Scotland. The route was first surveyed in 1733 by the Scottish engineer James Watt, pioneer of steam power, but it was nearly 90 years before the canal was opened. Its engineer was another famous Scot, Thomas Telford.

Inverness is a boom town; its economy and population are the fastest growing in Scotland and its suburbs have colonised the near hills and shores of its two fair firths, Moray and Beauly. It stands at the junction of several major routes

Ben Nevis at twilight. Scotland's highest mountain is a formidable presence, commanding the head of Loch Linnhe, the entrance to the Great Glen and the Road to the Isles.

through the glens and has been a hub of military manoeuvres and commercial traffic for many centuries; but there is no great sense of antiquity about the city today.

There has been a castle on the same site by the River Ness for at least 1000 years but the present fortress, an imposing red sandstone building which houses the law courts and municipal offices, dates back only to the 19th century. An earlier Inverness Castle was blown up by the Jacobite army of Charles Edward Stuart and its rubble was ignored until 1834, when the replacement was built. It is now the town's best-known landmark and presides over its most attractive area, where a network of riverside walks and footbridges crosses the water by way of Ness Islands to Eden Court Theatre, a cultural centre of the city.

Culloden Moor, site of the last battle to be fought on British soil, is only 8 km from the town. Scattered stones mark the Graves of the Clans – the ill-equipped Highland army cut down in 40 minutes by the heavy artillery of the British state. Bonnie Prince Charlie, after many adventures, escaped to France, leaving his Jacobite support in disarray and the Highland way of life fatally damaged. Today the National Trust for Scotland visitor centre makes a credible effort to describe this bitter conflict and the oppression of Gaelic Scotland which followed.

The Central Highlands' main road artery, the A9, bypasses melancholy Culloden on its route south to Strathspey and Aviemore, gateway to the Cairngorms. This is the land of the Whisky Trail, where visitors are invited to inspect the process of producing malt whisky. It's also the epicentre of organised leisure in the Highlands: ski-ing in the Cairngorms, kayaking and sailing on Loch Morlich and any number of forest trails and picnic sites. Aviemore, once a quiet granite village, is now the area's leading resort, and looks the part.

Strathspey is one of the loveliest river valleys in Scotland, as much celebrated for its angling as its malt whiskies. Its "capital" is Grantown-on-Spey which was an 18th-century "new town", planned and built by its local laird. Here the Highland landscape is tamed and gentled by natural woodland, open pastures and the clear waters of the Spey itself. The mountains are never far away, but you can view them in comfort from the steam train which runs along the Strathspey Railway during the summer months.

Efforts have been made to tame the Cairngorms too – or at least their most available mountain, Cairn Gorm itself. A lump of a hill, 1245 m high, it bears all the apparatus of the ski industry, and the more recently added funicular railway, which lifts less energetic tourists to a viewpoint on the mountain. Yet this high, inhospitable and often dangerous plateau, with its precipitous corries, ferocious winds and sudden storms, remains wild. It is almost as if the Cairngorms reject the very notion of such "soft" tourism.

There has been a fortress on this strategic headland on Loch Ness since the 12th century. Today the extensive ruins of Urquhart Castle are the loch's most visited site.

Loch Ness in golden mood. There have been no recent sightings of its "Monster" but the enigma remains.

Loch Ness

The earliest sighting of a monstrous presence in the Loch Ness area took place in the late 6th century. According to Adamnan, his biographer, the witness was none other than St Columba, the Irish monk credited with spreading Christianity into Scotland. The missionary was on an evangelical journey from his Iona community to the Pictish settlement which would become Inverness, when he asked a servant to swim across the River Ness to fetch a boat. Writing a century later, Adamnan described a giant creature which broke the surface of the water "with a great roar and open mouth", striking terror in the hearts of all but St Columba, who made the sign of the cross and commanded, "Think not to go further, nor touch that man. Quick, go back."

And it did. For the next 1400 years the beast disappeared from written history – if not oral tradition – until the "Loch Ness Monster" was more firmly delivered to an emerging age of mass communication. Rumours of the phenomenon began surfacing in the late 19th century, and gathered momentum throughout the 20th with the first photographs of sinuous necks, massive humps and mysterious wakes. Some were proved to be hoaxes, others remain inexplicable, like the sightings which proliferated when the main road along the loch was upgraded in the 1930s.

The monster, soon to be known as "Nessie", achieved international celebrity in 1933 when a reliable couple reported seeing "a most extraordinary form of animal", about eight metres long with a long, narrow, undulating neck like an elephant's trunk, cross the road in front of their car and lurch into the loch, leaving a trail of crushed vegetation behind. Thereafter the spectator sport of Nessie-hunting was here to stay.

Loch Ness has plenty of features to inflame the imagination; its notoriously murky water, discoloured by peat, has been plumbed to depths of 240 metres, and there is the suggestion that it has subterranean channels linking it to the sea. In 1933 the *Daily Mail* sponsored the first attempt to find Nessie with nothing more sophisticated than a boat, a big-game hunter and a photographer. Since then the hunt has continued with underwater cameras, observational submersibles, echo sounders, sonar scanners, NASA computers and all the expertise that advanced technology and natural science can deploy. Various baffling images of "large, unidentified objects" or "moving masses" in the depths of the loch have come and gone, and monster-believers use them to argue that the evidence is inconclusive. Is there such a thing as the Loch Ness Monster? As it's impossible to prove a negative the riddle remains unsolved.

With a few exceptions the scientific consensus considers Nessie a modern-day myth re-inforced by hoaxes, optical illusions, the misidentification of floating branches and common animals (seals, otters, swimming deer) and wishful thinking; which doesn't necessarily mean she has been ignored by scientists, who are happy to discuss theories about trapped populations of plesiosaurs or other prehistoric reptiles. In 2008 one of the most persistent researchers, Robert Rines of the Academy of Applied Sciences, even expressed the gloomy opinion that Nessie may have fallen victim to global warning, as there have been no reported sightings for some time.

As for St Columba – in the chronicles of saints it is common for them to be associated with monsters whom they overcome by the power of faith; what's more, the noisy, threatening beast showed behaviour never again repeated by shy, silent Nessie in any of her "sightings", and emerged from the River Ness, not the loch. But as long as there is the popular will to believe that a thrilling enigma, defying the best efforts of international science, remains unexplained in Loch Ness there will be life in its monster.

Inverness and the River Ness: the city centre riverbanks provide a focus for the cultural life of the Highland capital.
Cawdor Castle (opposite), begun in the 14th century, was the fortress of the Thanes of Cawdor, whose title was promised to Macbeth in Shakespeare's play.

107

The "Parallel Roads" of Glen Roy – three terraces left behind by the receding levels of an Ice Age loch.

Loch nam Faoileag (opposite), near Drumnadrochit – the tourist epicentre of Loch Ness and an important junction between Inverness and the south-west.

Scotch Whisky

Why whisky? The word is an Anglicisation of the Gaelic *uisge beatha*, which means "water of life." What is Scotch whisky? A distillate made in Scotland from cereals, water and yeast; in world markets it outsells every other noble spirit. There are two kinds: malt whisky, which is made from malted barley by the pot still process, and grain whisky, which is made from a mixture of malted and unmalted barely and other cereals by the patent still process. Blended whisky, which can be a blend of as many as 50 individual malt and grain whiskies, accounts for over 90 per cent of all Scotch sold globally. Single whiskies are products of a single distillery, and for connoisseurs the most prized of these are the single malts.

Today the industry is highly organised, highly regulated and a major contributor to the United Kingdom economy, but Scots have been distilling whisky less formally for many centuries. Some claim that Irish monks introduced the process to Scotland along with Christianity, but there's nothing to suggest that Highland farmers failed to discover for themselves how to distil spirit from their surplus barley. For perhaps as long as 1000 years this was a private business; the earliest reference to a distillery in the Acts of the Scottish Parliament was in 1690, and by that time Parliament had passed an Excise Act fixing duty on "aquavitae or other strong liquor.'"

Excise duty has been a sore grievance to whisky-drinkers ever since. After the Union of the Parliaments in 1707 English revenue staff crossed the border to bring whisky production under control, and there began a robust history of smuggling and illicit distilling. Many Scots took the reasonable view that they shouldn't be made to pay for the privilege of making their native drink. Eventually the industry and its tax regime evolved into the major business and revenue-earner we know today, but the "illicit still" flourished in the lonelier corners of the Highlands and Hebrides well into the 20th century. Who knows? One or two may survive yet.

Geography is less significant in the production of blended whisky, but the distilleries producing malt whiskies, with their more pronounced bouquets and individual flavours, have become landmarks on Scotland's tourist map. The malts are divided into five geographical groups: Lowland malts are made south of an imaginary line from Dundee in the east to Greenock in the west; Highland malts are made north of that line, including Orkney; Speyside malts form their own separate region; Islay malts are produced in the eight distilleries on the island of Islay; and – out on a limb – Campbeltown malts come from the town of Campbeltown, on the Mull of Kintyre.

Whisky-lovers all have their preferences. Malts vary in flavour according to their distillery, and real experts can source their provenance in blind tastings. The Lowland malts have the lightest characteristics, and the heaviest, whose famous names include Laphroaig, Bowmore, Lagavulin and Bunnahabhain, come from Islay; while the Speyside malts, including Glenlivet, Glen Grant, Glenfiddich and Cardhu, are a group distinctive from the Highland malts.

The mysterious influences which determine the flavours of different malts are not fully understood, but several factors are involved: critically a supply of quality barley and good soft water (generously produced by the Scottish climate), peat to fire the kiln or oven in which the malted barley is dried (a process which lends evocative smokiness to many malts) and the wisdom and experience of the "stillman" who controls the distilling process. All Scotch whiskies, grain or malt, have a flavour which has defied imitators throughout the world. The spirit is uniquely our "water of life", and we're keeping it that way.

Highland Park, Orkney

Glenfiddich, Speyside

Lagavulin, Islay

Dalmore, Highland

Late summer brings a plum-coloured bloom to the Cairngorms as the heather flowers around gem-like Loch an Eilein.
The highest and wildest mountain plateau in Britain, this wintry view of the Cairngorm massif (opposite) gives an idea of its scale.

The approach to Glen Coe from the east: Black Mount, a high stretch of moorland between Rannoch Moor and Glen Etive.
The Cairngorm foothills support remnants of the Great Wood of Caledon (opposite), the pine forest which once covered much of Scotland.

The Massacre of Glencoe

The name of this gloomy but spectacular glen has become synonymous with perfidy. Few visitors pass through the mountain gates of Glen Coe without feeling the weight of its intimidating landscape, as if the glen is reluctant to throw off its reputation. People continue to die here; the formidable peaks of Buachaille Etive Mòr, Bidean nam Bian and the ragged Aonach Eagach ridge take an annual toll of climbers, and loom over the road like a threat. But those who died in Glencoe on a winter morning in 1692 were not extreme sports enthusiasts, but victims of a covert Government plot driven by vicious Lowland prejudice.

There has been much historical myth-making about the Massacre of Glencoe, which was entirely the intention of those who planned it – the 17th-century spin doctors and establishment figures who helped create the popular belief that the mass murders were down to long-standing enmity between Clan Campbell and Clan MacDonald. To this day the Clachaig Inn in the village of Glencoe stokes the legend with a notice: "No hawkers or Campbells."

It is true that the military force sent to put the "miscreants" to the sword was a regiment recruited from the Campbell heartland of Argyll, and commanded by Captain Robert Campbell of Glenlyon, who had a grievance against the Maclains, a sept of the MacDonald clan. (Some years earlier they had looted his lands). But only a minority of the 120 Government soldiers had the name Campbell, many of the officers were Lowlanders and some were so appalled by the secret plot to attack the hospitable MacDonalds that they warned their hosts to flee. Two lieutenants even broke their swords and defied their orders.

It is, more than anything, the abuse of Highland hospitality which has made the massacre so infamous. By the standards of the day there was no exceptional loss of life: Alastair Maclain, the 12th Chief of Glencoe, and 37 of his clansmen were killed, the old chief as he rose from his bed; 40 women and children died of exposure after their homes were burned. But Captain Campbell, a Highlander himself, had defiled something sacred in Highland culture; treated as guests he and his men turned on their hosts.

Why were they there? The MacDonalds were Jacobites who had helped the efforts to restore the evicted King James II (James VII of Scotland) to the British throne, which was now occupied by William of Orange at the behest of the English Parliament. After the failure of this early Jacobite rebellion the Highland chiefs were ordered to swear an oath of loyalty to the new king, under threat of reprisal. They were given a deadline: January 1, 1692.

Maclain waited until the last moment but duly presented himself to the governor of Fort William, who sent him to Inveraray to take the oath. There followed a series of misadventures which made him miss the deadline by three days, but he was assured his loyalty had been registered. The chief returned to his glen with an easy heart. In Edinburgh, however, Sir John Dalrymple, the Scottish Secretary, and Sir Thomas Livingstone, commander of the army in Scotland, saw an opportunity to teach the "Highland barbarians" a lesson. King William was persuaded the MacDonalds had breached the terms of their pardon and signed the order to dispatch a regiment to Glencoe, where it was billeted on the clan communities.

Despite the conspirators' efforts to direct attention to tensions between Campbells and MacDonalds there was an outcry when the massacre became public, followed by an inquiry which judged the slaughter "murder." The king was exonerated and Dalrymple was held to blame, but no-one was brought to justice. The Massacre of Glencoe became a propaganda tool for the Jacobites when they made their more determined attempt to restore the Stuart dynasty in 1745. It is also another example of the Scottish appetite for tragic myths.

"The big herdsman of Etive" – Buachaille Etive Mòr – is the most spectacular mountain gatepost at the entrance to Glen Coe.

Heartlands of the Clans

THE WEST HIGHLANDS & ISLANDS

Between the deep fissure of Loch Linnhe and the mighty Torridon Mountains lie the seaboard and landscape which best express the romantic idea of Scotland: "O Caledonia! stern and wild…land of the mountain and the flood"; as promoted by Sir Walter Scott and successive generations of writers, painters, tourism entrepreneurs and marketing executives for everything Scottish from whisky to porridge oats. Here are the most spectacular mountain ranges, wildest glens, most dramatic castles, loneliest beaches, remotest islands, and, quite possibly, the purplest heather. This is the *Gaedhealechd* – the region of Scotland where Gaelic culture and language still survive, although diluted by emigration, immigration and the influence of global communications.

Despite the shiftiness of the West Highland climate, which brings the full force of Atlantic weather systems to the region, it never fails to beguile; and when the sun shines it is heartachingly beautiful, its intricate lacework of land and sea, soft colours and sharp edges like nowhere else in the world. There is poignancy, too, in its desolate places for those who know something of Scotland's history. But you can't take the Road to the Isles with anything other than a high heart.

This evocative highway begins at Fort William, an important Highland town with a celebrated neighbour: Ben Nevis, Scotland's highest mountain. Those with islands in their sights head west from the great Ben and skirt the Ardnamurchan peninsula with its landmark lighthouse – the most westerly point of mainland Britain. Their road follows the route of the West Highland Line, recently voted among the world's most beautiful rail journeys, to the port of Mallaig, where they can catch ferries to the Small Isles of Rum, Eigg, Muck and Canna, and the largest of the Inner Hebrides, Skye.

The spirit of Bonnie Prince Charlie – Charles Edward Stuart, claimant to the British throne – goes with them all the way. He arrived from France in the summer of 1745 to rally Jacobite support among the clans, raised his standard at Glenfinnan, south of Mallaig, and after nine months of jubilant victories, grim retreats and final defeat famously went "over the sea to Skye"; not from the mainland but from the Outer Hebrides,

In 1745 Charles Edward Stuart raised his standard at Glenfinnan to summon the support of the Jacobite clans, an event commemorated by the 19th-century monument at the head of Loch Sheil.

where the Prince went island-hopping to evade capture. Aided by the Skye heroine Flora MacDonald he escaped to permanent exile in France.

Few visit the islands without making Skye their priority, and although it's now linked to the mainland by a bridge across the Kyle narrows it's still possible to sail "over the sea" from Mallaig to Armadale. Even without its stirring history Skye is a commanding place, with the highest and most challenging mountain range in the British Isles: the Black Cuillin. On the east coast is the capital, Portree, with a pretty harbour in a deep bay; to the north are the curious hills of the Quiraing, with their "spires" of eroded rock; to the west is Dunvegan Castle, seat of the Clan MacLeod.

On clear days the Outer Hebrides line the horizon in a series of peaks and low-lying bumps, interrupted by narrow channels. Some of them are bridged by causeways, some linked by small car ferries, and the lands between are not for the faint-hearted; some visitors find their treeless moors and plains of peat bog intimidating; others relish their other-worldly isolation and the empty, shining beaches of their western seaboard. If it weren't for cold Atlantic breakers rolling in from Newfoundland and volatile weather, these beaches would be lined with hotels, as they are arguably the finest in Europe.

The largest island is Lewis, which is attached to its mountainous neighbour, Harris, by a neck of land. Its capital,

the port of Stornoway, is the only place that might be called urban on the entire chain, while the Harris Tweed industry maintains a precarious hold in the cottages of Harris. From there the islands spill southwards to the Uists, Benebecula and Barra, while 40 miles out in the Atlantic is the western extremity of Europe: St Kilda, a precipitous island group now a World Heritage Site for the relics of the unique community who once lived there. Sustainable life became so untenable for the St Kildans that in the 1930s they asked to be evacuated to the mainland.

Most of the island ports have ferry links with either Skye or Oban, but Stornoway has its own route to the mainland at Ullapool, on Loch Broom, where the landscape is among the most majestic in Scotland. This is Wester Ross, its coast penetrated by long, narrow sea lochs and fractured into jutting peninsulas which, until the 20th century, could be reached only by boat or on foot. Today Wester Ross has a low-key tourist infrastructure; its white-washed villages are charming, its beaches unblemished and its seaboard mountains, the magnificent Torridon peaks, stir the blood.

Inland, where Wester Ross reaches cross-country to Sutherland and Inverness-shire, there is another wild wedge of land, defined by empty glens, island-studded lochs and the loneliest hills in Scotland. The most beautiful of its more accessible spots are Loch Maree and Glen Affric.

Since the Kyle narrows were bridged, Skye may have technically lost its island status, but its romance is undiminished and its drama endures in this Cuillin view from Gesto Bay.

Highland Games

The origins of Highland Games are obscured by the kind of mist which all too often attends these summer highlights of the Caledonian year. There are well over 100 gatherings held between mid-May and mid-September, and their numbers have steadily grown since the 1820s, when the Victorians discovered a romantic enthusiasm for all things Highland and revived the tradition, which had almost disappeared from the land of the clans when Gaelic culture was suppressed after the Jacobite Rebellion of 1745.

Like many forms of competitive sport the early games were a means of encouraging the skills and strengths required for war. The kingly name of Malcolm Canmore is often cited as a founding member, as he organised a race up a mountain called Craig Choinich, near Braemar, to choose a foot-messenger who was rewarded with a baldric, or warrior's belt. The Craig Choinich race is repeated today at the Braemar Gathering, which has been attended by the Royal Family ever since Queen Victoria built her holiday home at nearby Balmoral.

Malcolm is also credited with inventing the sword dance. When he slew a chieftain of his enemy Macbeth, he crossed his sword with his own on the ground and did a little jig before returning to the fray. But the Fife village of Ceres also claims to have held the first games three centuries later, when victorious Scottish bowmen returned from Bannockburn in 1314. The Ceres games certainly have a long pedigree, and if their Lowland venue seems curious there are actually many other games south of the Highland fault line. Today there are games in the Lanarkshire town of Shotts, a former mining community, the Ayrshire port of Ardrossan and the Glasgow suburb of Bearsden and Milngavie, to name but a few Lowland events.

Wherever they are held, Highland Games are occasions which maintain the traditions of piping, dancing, heavy events and field and track with real passion. Even on the dullest of summer days they are pageants of colour and vitality, with the entire spectrum of tartan patterns on parade and the sound of the bagpipes – massed or solo – rarely absent. To purists, solo pipers are the aristocrats and win the highest honours and biggest prizes, but the average crowd favours the heavy events: tossing the caber, putting the shot, and throwing the hammer.

In these activities it's easy to see how early competitors took part in trials of strength and skill with whatever came to hand: a tree trunk, now tapered, with a regulation length of six metres and 57 kg, is the caber which must be upended and tossed to the perpendicular; a blacksmith's hammer evolved into the heavy hammer which is thrown by its wooden shaft as far as possible; and a big stone became the shot putt which must do the same.

Highland dancing, once practised exclusively by men, is now dominated by teenage girls and children, some as young as three or four. The odd boy might put in an appearance to dance the Highland Fling, which was inspired, according to one story, by the flourishing antlers of rutting stags. A grandfather playing his pipes on the hills encouraged his young grandson to dance along, and when he saw two stags on the horizon with their antlers lifted against the sky he instructed, "Raise your hands above your head like the horns o' they stags." The Highland Fling, which is always performed on one spot, is also said to have been danced traditionally on a shield.

The venues of games are chosen more for their scenic value than their sporting facilities. The largest in Scotland is the Cowal Highland Gathering, which takes place in Dunoon, on the Clyde estuary, with an annual entry of about 3500 competitors and up to 20,000 spectators. But wherever in the world you find more than a handful of Scots you find Highland Games. The largest in the northern hemisphere is the mighty gathering of the New Caledonian Club of San Francisco, which has been held annually since 1865 and attracts crowds of between 50,000 and 100,000.

Glen Affric is one of three long glens which reach deep into the Northern Highlands – and the most beautiful.

Plockton, on a peninsula near the mouth of Loch Carron, Wester Ross, has a mild climate influenced by the Gulf Stream.
Empty white sand but volatile weather: the scattered houses of Gairloch (opposite) a former fishing village in Wester Ross.

Beinn Eighe, seen here from Loch Clair, is one of the magnificent Torridon mountain triptych of Beinn Eighe, Beinn Alligan and Liathach.
Studded with wooded islands, Loch Maree (opposite) may take its name from St. Maol Rubha who founded a monastery at Applecross in the 7-8th century.

The district of Kintail at the head of Loch Duich is defined by its shapely mountains – the Five Sisters of Kintail.

Now restored, the 13th-century fortress of Eilean Donan (opposite) on Loch Duich was for centuries a stronghold of the MacKenzies and MacRaes of Kintail.

The Clan System

The Gaelic word clann means "children of the family". Pre-Christian social organisation in Ireland and Scotland was based on the extended family, theoretically all descended from one person, whose bonds evolved into a system whereby the protection of the family patriarch – the clan chief – was reciprocated by obligations from those who claimed kinship. Traditions of heritage and allegiance were part of both Celtic and Norse cultures, but by the 12th and 13th centuries the Highland clans had also taken on features of Norman feudalism.

Not all clans are Highland. There are Borders and Lowland clans – the Armstrongs, the Maxwells, the Turnbulls – who only became known as "families" in the 19th century. Their structure was similar, although they didn't come with the dress and language of the Gael, and they shared the appetite for territorial disputes and long-running feuds which gave the clans their unruly reputation. Until the 17th century, reiving – raiding the livestock of rival clans – was a rite of passage for all junior clansmen.

The clans' own processes of arbitration were quite sophisticated, and there was status to be found in family lineage. Clan Gregor, whose motto is "My Race is Royal", claimed descent from Kenneth MacAlpine, who in AD 832 became the first King of Alba (the early name for Scotland) while the MacDonalds and MacDougalls are descendants of the Lords of the Isles, who presided over the Hebrides and West Highland seaboard for four centuries.

By the 17th century clan chiefs had become landlords, with their "tacksmen" performing the role of factor, managing the chief's property and collecting rents from tenant crofters. It was also the tacksman's duty to summon the Clan Host for celebrations like weddings and games, but also for war; and with the Jacobite rebellions between the late 17th and mid 18th centuries the Highland clans, who largely supported the deposed Stuart dynasty, launched an era which ended in the dissolution of their way of life.

After the final rout of Jacobite resistance at Culloden the young British state, born of the controversial union of Scottish and English parliaments in 1707, exacted a revenge which amounted to cultural genocide. The wearing of tartan, the speaking of Gaelic and the right to bear arms were proscribed, and with new military roads and forts throughout the Highlands the British government did its best to crush the *Gaedhealechd*, dismantle the clan system and emasculate the power of the chiefs, paving the way for the forced evictions and mass emigrations which sent thousands of Gaels overseas, notably to Canada and America.

The ironic sting in this melancholy tale is that less than 50 years later, after the repeal of the Dress Act, there was a flowering of romantic interest in the Highlands. Aristocratic "Highland Societies" were formed to promote Highland culture and dress, especially tartan. Woven plaid had always been part of the clan wardrobe, produced to various designs by local weavers with an identification which was purely regional. But the association of different tartans with different clans only arrived as a "fashion statement" in the early 19th century, when the Highland Society of London began naming clan-specific tartans. The seal of approval on the fabric was set by George IV, who was kitted out in Royal Stuart tartan for his state visit to Edinburgh in 1822 – an event masterminded by Sir Walter Scott, whose novels also inspired new pride in Scotland.

Today clan chiefs have no legal authority but hold a title of honour, recognised by the sovereign. The clan system has also gone global. The traditions of heritage and allegiance have become the founding principles of an international social club which maintains the roots of the Scottish diaspora, while the tartans of the clans have become Scotland's corporate colours. We do well to remember at what cost.

Mountainous Rùm and flat topped Eigg, with its jutting escarpment, are two of the island group called the Small Isles.

The Cuillin hills at their most fearsome crowd the skies near the village of Elgol on the south-east coast of Skye.

Staffin crofthouses, on the Trotternish peninsula of Skye. Above them is the Quiraing, a curious landscape of landslips and eroded rock.

Skye's towering Old Man of Storr, and lesser neighbours, can be reached from the road between Portree and Staffin.

Neist Point (opposite) on the Waternish peninsula is the most westerly headland in Skye. Its lighthouse, dating from 1909, is now automated.

Many of the islands in the Outer Hebrides are now linked by causeways, like this one between Benebecula and North Uist.

Sands of the tiny island of Berneray, off North Uist (opposite). The Outer Hebrides justifiably claim to have the finest beaches in Scotland.

On a windswept moor in north Lewis, the stone circle of Calanais is among the most complete prehistoric sites in Britain.
Tràigh Seilebost and Luskentyre, South Harris (opposite), have shorelines with spectacular flat sands, dunes and machair.

Old Stones of the Norse Lands

NORTHERN SCOTLAND, ORKNEY & SHETLAND

Scotland reclaims its wildness as you travel to its northern edge, and is reluctant to vanish into the cold wastes of sea which stretch all the way to the Arctic Circle. Beyond the mainland are the two island groups which have always been ambiguous about their Scottishness, Orkney and Shetland. In the south is Easter Ross, where there is a last flourish of towns and villages before the land empties into the desolation of central Caithness and Sutherland. To the west are the strange, free-standing mountains of Assynt. To the east is a series of firths, and some confusing geography.

The Black Isle is neither black nor an island (no one knows for sure how it got its name) but a peninsular hump of productive land between the Moray and Cromarty firths. Farther north, the Dornoch Firth is unexpectedly festive with its holiday sands, caravan parks and golf links; and Dornoch itself is a handsome little town built of golden sandstone, with a medieval cathedral. But this welcoming stretch of coast is the lull before an old storm which has never quite subsided.

Northwards the titanic statue of the First Duke of Sutherland signals the gateway to the depopulated Sutherland interior.

From then on the population clings to the shoreline in a sparse line of villages until it comes together in the Caithness capital of Wick, once home port to a 1000-strong herring fleet and, much earlier, part of the fief of the Vikings. John o' Groats, a rambling village, is popularly believed to be the most northerly point of the British mainland but is overtaken by Dunnet Head, near Thurso, just 10 km across the Pentland Firth from the Orkney archipelago. Only 16 of Orkney's 67 islands are inhabited. Most are low-lying and fertile, the highest is Hoy, which has the loftiest cliffs in Britain, and the largest is Mainland, where you find much of Orkney's rich heritage, including the densest concentration of prehistoric monuments in Britain.

Here is nirvana for anyone with a passion for the distant past. The Stone Age village of Skara Brae – the most complete Neolithic monument in Europe – is a complex of

Freestanding Suilven is something of an icon to lovers of the haunting Assynt landscape. It is not the highest mountain in Sutherland but demanding to climb for its isolation.

drystone houses 5000 years old. The islands are littered with burial cairns and standing stones, including the impressive chambered tomb of Maes Howe and the Ring of Brodgar, whose monoliths pose like models on their coastal site. Orkney's capital, Kirkwall, is a port with a magnificent centrepiece of three medieval buildings: St Magnus Cathedral, raised from local sandstone in the 12th century, and the Bishop's Palace and Earl's Palace, the fortified homes (now ruins) of Norse churchmen and nobles.

Orkney became part of Scotland only in 1468; for more than five centuries it belonged to a sea empire founded by Norwegian kings, whose colonists left behind a vigorous race with a unique dialect shot through with Norse words. Shetland has maintained its Norse heritage even more energetically. The two island groups are separated by 96 km and although they have much in common – almost treeless landscapes bewilderingly entangled with the sea – their dialects, economy and sense of identity are distinctively different. Shetland lacks the gentling green of Orkney; its peaty uplands are unproductive and it has always relied more heavily on harvesting the sea – including, more recently, the oil beneath the sea. The huge terminal of Sullom Voe receives half of Britain's oil production.

The port capital of Lerwick has strong links with Scandinavia and the Baltic states, and its traffic lends an unexpected internationalism to this sturdy grey town. But the event which attracts most visitors is the annual fire festival of Up Helly Aa, when Shetlanders celebrate their Viking past. This is very much an authentic tradition inspired by pagan sun worship. It's held each January to welcome the cautious return of light to the northern winter, and its climax takes place at the harbour, where a procession of latterday "Vikings" convenes to ignite a replica galley.

The northern seaboard of Caithness and Sutherland has all the drama of a Norse saga. Between Duncansby Head in the east and Cape Wrath in the west the coast is a sweep of cliffs, gorges, sea stacks and bays, and its hinterland is the emptiest in Scotland – vast plains of rusty peatland and bog punctuated by isolated mountains. Despite the waters boiling round the headland of Cape Wrath its name comes from the Norse word *hvarf*, which means turning point, and when the coast takes a hard left south the land of the Viking begins to fuse with the land of the Gael.

The western seaboard picks up its ragged theme of sea lochs, fishing harbours and offshore islands until it plunges into the hills at Loch Broom and the tourist hub of Ullapool; more a large village than a small town, but with its long waterfront of white-painted cottages, hotels, restaurants and gift shops it seems almost metropolitan after the remote settlements which have gone before.

Once the main herring fishing port of the west coast, Ullapool is now better known as a tourist centre for its prime situation on Loch Broom and ferry to Stornoway.

Ardvreck Castle, on Loch Assynt, is a relic of the Macleods of Assynt, who held terrorities here for over 300 years.

Loch Inchard (opposite): this Sutherland loch lies close to Laxford Bridge – a name which derives from the Norse for salmon.

The Clearances

The Highland Clearances are notorious in a way that similar "reforms" in the Lowlands and England are not. South of the border the agricultural revolution began in the 17th century with enclosures of land which drove much of the rural population into cities. Scotland's clearances came later; in the Lowlands from about 1760 to 1830, when new systems of agriculture forced thousands of country people to seek work in the growing industrial centres of Glasgow, Edinburgh and Dundee; in the Highlands from about the same time until the 1870s.

All these migrations caused social disruption, but the Highland Clearances have greater infamy for several reasons: the abrupt dismantling of clan structures and their support systems, the lack of legal protection for year-by-year tenants under Scots law, and the callousness which some landlords – among them clan chiefs – pursued the evictions. All combined to empty the Highlands of much of its indigenous population and inflict near-fatal damage on the language and culture of the Gael.

There's no doubt that by the 18th century the Highlands were overpopulated and, as a result, chronically poor; that the semi-feudal clan system was an anachronism crying out for reform. But in the aftermath of the Jacobite Rebellion of 1745 its Highland supporters suffered retribution which systematically sought to change their way of life and turned many of the chiefs, who lost their paternalism with their power, into self-seeking landlords. Their "improvements" began with sheep

**Old crofthouse at Strathyokel,
in the empty heart of Sutherland.**

farming, and the introduction of the hardy blackface and Cheviot breeds which could cope with mountain weather. As the Clearances gathered momentum the year 1792 became known as The Year of the Sheep.

It and the years that followed are remembered in the ghosts of townships whose old stones push through heather and turf in the glens today; most bitterly in Sutherland, where families were forced to leave their crops in the ground while their homes were burned around them. "Little or no time was given for the removal of persons or property," wrote one crofter witness, Donald McLeod, who counted 250 burning houses; "the people striving to remove the sick and helpless before the fire should reach them." The brutality of the Sutherland clearances, enforced by the Countess of Sutherland, her husband the First Duke and their avaricious factor Patrick Sellar, still scars the memories of some local people.

Some landlords did offer optional land: usually unproductive coastal strips. Others simply pointed their tenants in the direction of the emigration ships whose passenger lists became a Gaelic diaspora. Their main destinations were Nova Scotia, Ontario and the American colonies. The potato famine of 1846 precipitated a second wave of emigration to North America, Australia and New Zealand, where pockets of Gaelic culture survive. In Scotland the language is still being rescued from extinction.

The most emotive critics of the Clearances have described them as a form of ethnic cleansing, but the Gaels were displaced by fellow Gaels as well as fellow Scots. The cleansing of the Highlands can't be called ethnic, but there's a good argument for calling it cultural.

Ben Kilbreck: this isolated mountain is all the more impressive for its solitary position on the moorland of central Sutherland.

Duncansby Head is the north-east extremity of mainland Scotland. The cliffs here have been splintered into sea stacks by fierce seas. The austere northern coast of Sutherland is relieved by glorious beaches. This is Strathy Bay (opposite), between Durness and Tongue.

The hills of Hoy, Orkney's highest island, rise behind the Standing Stones of Stenness, on the freshwater Loch of Harray.
Kirkwall (opposite), Orkney's capital, dates back to Norse times, when the Viking colonists also made it their capital.

Yesnaby, on Mainland, provides one of Orkney's many coastal spectacles when tempestous sea confronts defiant cliffs.

The red sandstone "Old Man of Hoy" (opposite) on the island of Hoy, is as high as St Paul's Cathedral and a favourite terminus of clifftop walks.

A replica Viking Galley is burned every year by Shetland's 'Viking jarls' at the winter fire festival of Up Helly Aa held in Lerwick.

The Vikings

Rapacious pirates in horned helmets? Noble Norsemen in winged headgear? The Viking reputation is shrouded in myth, perhaps because these Scandinavian expansionists and expert navigators were themselves eager to present their history in heroic form through the medium of the Norse saga. In fact, the everyday Viking helmet was conical, wingless and hornless, although its more spectacular version may have been used ceremonially, and for every foreign coast the Vikings raided there were others where they arrived as peaceful trading partners.

Their maritime activities were adventurous, and between the late 8th and early 11th century their explorers, warriors, merchants and pirates colonised wide areas of Europe, with their famous longships travelling as far as Constantinople and the Volga River in Russia, as well as Faroe, Iceland, Greenland, Newfoundland and Labrador. This was the Viking Age, and it had a profound impact on one of Norway's nearest neighbours. In the 9th century, before Scotland had become a united country, new settlers began arriving in Orkney and Shetland, putting down among the native Picts the roots of an independent Norse earldom which lasted six centuries.

The northern extremities of mainland Scotland were part of this sea empire, and Vikings also colonised the Inner and Outer Hebrides, Kintyre and the Isle of Man. But their most enduring seat of power was Orkney, where Kirkwall became the only Norse-age town of any importance in Britain. There, after Christian faith reached the pagan Vikings, a magnificent cathedral was raised and named for an 11th-century Norse nobleman martyred for his unfashionably charitable version of Christianity. Magnus's story is told in the Orkneyinga Saga, a series of tales first recited and then written down by an unknown author. He was killed "for good reasons of state" when, during a long-running feud with his cousin, he tried to practice the Christian principle of forgiveness.

St Magnus' Cathedral thrives today, surrounded by the remnants of palatial premises once occupied by Norse bishops and earls. Most ancient place-names in Orkney derive from Old Norse, and although the ancient stones of Kirkwall were quarried locally the original town plan is Norwegian. Shetland shares a similar legacy but the more northerly islands were never the earls' headquarters, and in 1195, during one of their many disputes with Norway, Orkney's earls were stripped of their Shetland possessions. By this time the Scottish north was beginning to lose touch with its origins and identify more with the rest of Scotland, and when King Hakon Hakonsson tried to re-assert dominance over his Scottish outposts in 1263, his campaign was disastrous. He died in Kirkwall the following winter.

From then all the earls of Orkney were Scots, but the Viking legacy lasted longer in the north than in other parts of the country, where long-running tensions between Norway and Scotland came to a head on the Ayrshire coast near Largs. Here Hakon confronted the army of Alexander III, who was determined to bring the Hebrides and Kintyre under the sovereignty of the Scottish crown.

His predecessor, Alexander II, had tried unsuccessfully to buy these territories from Norway, which had controlled them through vassal kings since about 1100. When the third Alexander was again refused the Scots began a series of raids on the Isle of Skye. Hakon responded with a mighty war fleet of longships. The Battle of Largs is generally agreed to have been indecisive, but storms and shipwrecks drove the Norwegians to Orkney, where their king's death ended the war and paved the way for negotiations. In 1266 both countries signed the Treaty of Perth and – for a fee – Scotland recovered the lands of the Gael. Orkney and Shetland, however, remained tributary to Norway until 1468, when they were ceded to King James III by Christian I of Denmark, who had inherited the Norse dominions, in lieu of a dowry which couldn't be paid.

155

Esha Ness: this headland on a mile of stupendous cliffs on Shetland's West Mainland receives the full force of Atlantic weather.
The mighty natural sea arch of Dore Holm (opposite) is one of Shetland's finest. It too endures the relentless assault of the waves.

Jarlshof is the best known prehistoric archaeological complex in Shetland. It represents five ages of occupation dating from the Bronze Age.
At the end of Scotland: St Ninian's Isle and tombolo (opposite), site of the discovery, in 1958, of a magnificent hoard of 8th-century Celtic Silver.

Index of Places

Fresh from the sea, Isle of Mull.